WEAVE | WRAP | COIL
creating artisan wire jewelry JODI BOMBARDIER

INTERWEAVE
interweave.com

EDITOR jean campbell

TECHNICAL EDITOR jean campbell

ART DIRECTOR liz quan

DESIGN karla baker

PHOTOGRAPHY joe coca

ILLUSTRATION bonnie brooks

PRODUCTION katherine jackson

INTERWEAVE PRESS LLC
201 EAST FOURTH STREET
LOVELAND, CO 80537
INTERWEAVE.COM

Printed in China by Asia Pacific Offset Ltd.

Library of Congress Cataloging-in-Publication Data
Bombardier, Jodi.
  Weave, wrap, coil : creating artisan wire jewelry / [Jodi Bombardier].
    p. cm.
  ISBN 978-1-59668-200-9 (pbk.)
  1. Jewelry making. 2. Wire jewelry. I. Title.
  TT212.B65 2010
  745.594'2--dc22
                              2010029890

10 9 8 7 6 5 4 3 2 1

dedication

MY LIFE'S GREATEST ACCOMPLISHMENTS—
JOANNA, JULES, AND JOEY. LOVE YOU.

contents

PROJECTS
beginner

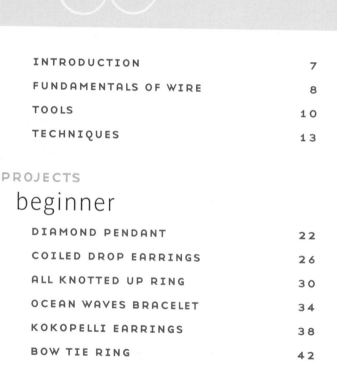

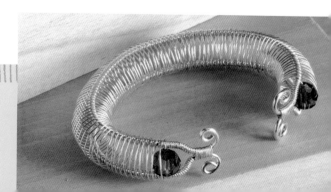

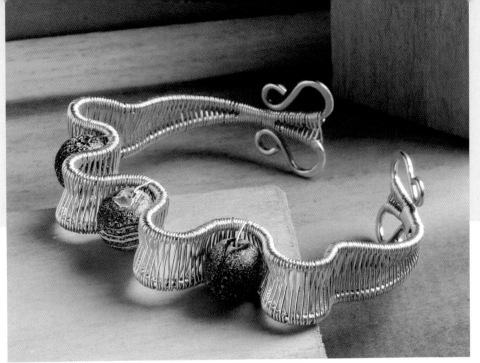

intermediate

advanced

INTRODUCTION

I started my jewelry-making career with memory wire, switched to stringing, then tried chain mail. All the while I saw pictures of wire-wrapped jewelry in various magazines and kept thinking, "That is the coolest thing ever. I've got to learn how to do that!" With the help of Mark Lareau's book, *All Wired Up*, I was ready to begin my adventure into the wonderment of wire wrapping.

I've been working with craft, copper, brass, and sterling silver wire for a number of years; long enough that I've been dubbed "The Wire Bender" by my children. There's something about wire that truly intrigues me to continuously search for new ways to weave, coil, texture, and twist it into unique pieces of jewelry. My inspiration for design comes mostly from other man-made objects such as a scroll on a fence or the unique architecture of a building. To me, wire is a line and the world is made up of endless lines, so I feel I'm surrounded by inspiration.

So how did I start weaving with wire? Well, I love baskets. At one point, I had so many baskets that I had to thin out my collection because they were taking over my home. My love for baskets got me thinking, "I should figure out how to make craft wire baskets," so off to the library I went to check out books on basketmaking and weaving. Reading through those books certainly was helpful, but I still had to devise a way to make it work with wire . . . sometimes the simplest thing can seem so challenging!

After several trials and errors, I finally came up with a technique that was easy and effective, and as I made one little basket after another, I realized I had to transition this newfound wire skill to jewelry. Such was the beginning of endless ideas and a new avenue to travel with wire.

In *Weave Wrap Coil*, I primarily teach the fundamentals of weaving and coiling. Coiled jewelry has longtime been a popular look in the wire world, but weaving is a great extension of coiling, so I believe it will become the hot new trend! The projects utilize variations of the same weave as well as introduce a basketweave. A slight variation in a weave pattern can lead to many new ideas that all have a fresh look of their own.

You'll soon discover that the projects in this book are sorted into three categories: beginner, intermediate, and advanced. They incorporate weaving, coiling, wire wrapping, forging, filing/sanding, or a mixture of the techniques. The trick to many of these techniques is to understand how to work with 26-gauge wire; there's definitely some finesse required, but with a little patience, the payoff is big. In order to understand which projects might work best for you, here are the category definitions:

BEGINNER: This level project is written with basic design structure, teaching rudimentary weaving and coiling to the novice designer. There will be no mystery for an intermediate or advanced level designer regarding construction for these pieces.

INTERMEDIATE: These projects are for someone with basic weaving, coiling, and wire-wrapping skills, but who needs some guidance on construction. An intermediate project is not a construction mystery to the advanced designer. The advanced designer may need to skim the instructions or illustrations of an intermediate project, but more than likely, an advanced designer can look at the project and have an understanding of construction.

ADVANCED: The construction of advanced projects will stump this level designer because there is a "mystery" in how the project is constructed that is not readily visible.

I hope *Weave Wrap Coil* will be just the inspiration you need to get you on your way to making beautifully finished jewelry. With its variety of projects and technique levels, it truly has something for everyone. Enjoy!

FUNDAMENTALS OF WIRE

I saw a T-shirt once that stated one can never have enough beads, but in my world, one can never have enough wire! I work with sterling silver, copper (my favorite to work with), craft, and brass wire. This chapter will give you a foundation of wire properties that every wireworker needs to know before getting started.

Wire Gauges

Wire comes in a large range of diameters, or gauges. When looking at the American Standard Wire Gauge, the smallest gauge is 38 and the largest is 1. The first thing that pops into my mind is, "Why are the numbers backward; 1 the largest and 38 the smallest?" There's actually a good reason. The gauge relates to the number of times the wire is pulled through holes in steel plates. Each time the wire gets pulled, it goes through a smaller hole to reach the desired gauge. Theoretically, that means that 28-gauge wire is pulled through steel plates 28 times to get it that small. For projects in this book, you'll primarily be working with round-profile wire ranging from 26- to 16-gauge.

Wire Hardness

Wire is available in different tensile strengths:

DEAD-SOFT OR SOFT: This wire is very malleable and easy to work with.

HALF-HARD: This wire has some stiffness to it.

HARD: This is very rigid wire.

I only use dead-soft wire as the weaving and coiling wire for the projects in this book. Dead-soft wire is perfect for weaving and coiling because its malleability and flexibility allows for weaving and coiling in, out, and around thicker-gauged wire frames.

I also use dead-soft wire in larger gauges. When coiling rings, for example, half-hard would be quite challenging to coil to shape the ring frame because it is "springy," while dead-soft is not as springy. When shaping wire frames, dead-soft wire is just easier to shape and bend. Keep in mind that the larger the wire gauge used, the stiffer the wire is because of its thick diameter, even though it's dead-soft. Also, some wire by nature is harder than others. Dead-soft sterling silver is a bit stiffer than copper and craft wire and dead-soft brass wire is stiffer than all three. Dead-soft fine silver is extremely soft, much too soft to use for the book projects, especially for frames.

Sometimes wire does need to be work-hardened. Hooks, clasps, and arches of spirals are good examples of pieces that you might want to work-harden. If just working with the wire doesn't naturally make your wire hard enough, use a rawhide hammer to work-harden it, or use a goldsmith's hammer to texture, flatten, and work-harden the wire all at the same time.

Ultimately, the decision about whether to use dead-soft or half-hard wire depends on what you are creating and/or what you prefer to work with.

Wire Types

Wire comes in just about every kind of metal. I use two kinds the wires listed below in *Weave Wrap Coil*:

BRASS WIRE: Two colors of brass wire are available, red and yellow. I prefer the coloring of red brass over yellow. I find that brass is the most difficult wire to work with, as it is more stiff than copper, craft, and sterling silver wire. The stiffness makes it more springy. When wire is springy, it tends to curl more and curls lead to kinks.

COPPER WIRE: Copper wire is a wonderful wire to work with. It's cost effective and very malleable. Copper wire can potentially vary in coloration from one spool to the next. One time I was making a cuff, ran out of wire, and started a new spool. Once the cuff was complete, the color variation in the wire was quite apparent!

CRAFT WIRE: This readily available wire is made from coated copper. Craft wire doesn't tarnish since it's coated with colored plastic.

STERLING SILVER: This type of wire is 92.5% silver and 7.5% copper. The copper component in sterling silver causes the tarnishing effect.

I use copper, brass, and craft wire for making mock-ups or any time I'm making a new design because these wires are lower in cost than sterling silver. However, I also use copper, brass, and craft wire in many finished projects. Copper and brass are stunning with the right beads and craft wire offers such a wonderful variety in color, how can one resist it?

Another consideration in wire selection is the final cost of the jewelry piece you're making. Woven jewelry can be time-consuming and when calculating the price of any jewelry piece, you need to be justly compensated for your time. In my experience, the largest part of the price with woven jewelry is the time, not the material.

Safety

The number one rule in working with wire is to use common sense. When cutting wire, for example, you create a sharp edge with the cut. In addition to this, when you snip the wire, it literally becomes a projectile missile. Be smart! Just cup your hand over the wire as you cut it to keep the wire piece from flying across the room. If desired, you can lightly file the wire end to smooth the sharp edge cut.

Cleanliness

Work with clean hands. Natural body oils, lotions, and creams will only help dirty and tarnish your wire, not to mention make it harder to hold onto. If you're not going to antique your finished project, clean your wire thoroughly before using it. I like to use disposable jewelry cloths to clean my wire.

Straightening Your Wire

You'll typically purchase wire coiled or on a spool. You can straighten the wire as you clean it with a jewelry cloth or by using a nylon-jaw pliers (see page 10).

Precious Metal Scraps

Keep your fine metal scraps in a closeable container, not a plastic baggie, as the wire ends will poke through, and you'll lose your pieces. These scraps are not garbage but can be sold back to a refiner. Refiners can be found online through your favorite search engine.

Storage

Storing wire in plastic bags is an option for keeping several different gauges and types of wire organized. This also cuts down on tarnish. I store my wire in plastic bags, then in a plastic container that can hold hanging folders. I then label each folder with the type of wire and gauge.

Likewise, storing finished wire jewelry in plastic bags also greatly slows down the tarnishing effect and keeps your jewelry cleaner in general. Woven copper, brass, and sterling silver jewelry can be tumbled. Trying to clean woven jewelry with wipes is not possible as the jewelry is three-dimensional. I tumble woven pieces in stainless steel shot and soap, and they clean up beautifully!

TOOLS

Many of the projects in this book can be completed with minimal tools, but it is always a good idea to have a nice selection of tools on hand to help simplify what you are trying to accomplish, which is to make beautiful jewelry.

Wire Cutters

A sharp pair of wire cutters (also called flush cutters) is essential to getting nice, clean cuts on your wire. Flush cutters create both flush and pinch cuts when cutting the wire, leaving one end of the wire with a pinch cut and the other end with a flush cut. One side of the cutters creates the pinch cut, while the other side, the flat side, creates a straight, or flush cut.

Chain- and Flat-nose Pliers

Chain-nose and flat-nose pliers are used to hold wire and jewelry and also for making bends in wire. Chain-nose pliers are tapered and come to a point, while flat-nose pliers are straight and square off at the tip. Because the chain-nose pliers are narrow and taper, they are a better choice to use with weaving to get into really small, tight areas. A flat-nose pliers would simply be too wide. However, a flat-nose pliers is the tool of choice for making bends in wire since its barrel is squared.

Round-nose Pliers

Round-nose pliers are used to make loops and jump rings. Round-nose pliers can be purchased in a variety of barrel sizes. I have three pair: small, medium, and large. It's not necessary to have three sizes of pliers for the projects in this book, but it might be worth investing in them at some point. It's nice to have a choice of sizes with which to work. Mandrels (see page 11) are a handy substitute when you want to make a larger loop than what your pliers will make.

Parallel Pliers

Parallel pliers are similar to chain- and flat-nose pliers, but the barrels of the pliers close parallel to each other, instead of in a bird-bill-type fashion. They can be used to hold wire frames together or to straighten frames that are aligned cockeyed.

Nylon-jaw Pliers

This type of pliers is great for straightening wire. When possible, I use my nylon-jaw pliers to hold jewelry and open/close loops instead of using chain- or flat-nose pliers. This avoids leaving tool marks on my jewelry. Sometimes it's not possible to hold jewelry with nylon-jaw pliers, as the metal will slip within the pliers, but I always try the nylon-jaw pliers first.

Nylon-jaw Bracelet-forming Pliers

I absolutely love these pliers! A bracelet mandrel is a handy shaping tool, but the nylon-jaw bracelet-forming pliers is a superior tool for precisely shaping woven and coiled wire bracelets. To use them, just gently squeeze the cuff/bracelet, starting at one end, and work your way to the opposite end.

Mandrels

Mandrels, straight cylinders used for curving and bending wire, can open up the door on your creative imagination! Steel mandrels can be purchased at hardware stores. Other options include permanent markers, ballpoint pens, crochet hooks, and knitting needles. Markers and pens are great to use when round-nose pliers aren't quite large enough for a project.

Permanent Marker

Many times it is necessary to mark wire at certain lengths for the projects in this book. The marks can be rubbed off with a soft cotton or disposable jewelry cleaner cloth.

Low-stick Tape

When working with multiple pieces of wire at one time, it's very helpful to tape the pieces that are not being worked. At times, taping is also helpful to keep wires in place and to avoid getting bends in wire. Low-stick tape is typically found in hardware stores.

Stick Pin and Yarn Needle

Stick pins and yarn needles are useful little tools in separating wire, lifting wire up that has been pushed inward, or to hide wire ends. Yarn needles have a larger diameter than stick pins but don't have a sharp pointed end. Yarn needles are great to use when weaving in small spaces, which is discussed in Weaving in Small Spaces (page 19).

Polishing Cloths

Polishing cloths are great for cleaning wire. The cloth can do two things at once: clean the wire while you are straightening it. These cloths are disposable and come with a cleaning chemical on them. Typically as metal is cleaned, the cloth turns gray/black, using up the chemical.

Goldsmith's Hammer

I like to use a rounded-end goldsmith's hammer for texturing and forging as opposed to a flat-ended hammer that can leave gouges in the metal. A goldsmith's hammer can be purchased already rounded or with a flat head; you can determine if you want to round it yourself on a grinding wheel or leave it flat. I always buy my goldsmith's hammers already rounded.

Anvil or Metal Block

Anvils and metal blocks come in a large variety of shapes and sizes. For the projects in my book, a small metal block is sufficient. The one I use is 2½" (6.4 cm) square and about 1" (2.5 cm) thick.

Metal Files

Metal files are used to file out tool marks created when forging and for filing sharp edges created when cutting wire. I have two sets of metal files, a 4" (10.2 cm) long set and 6" (15.2 cm) long set. The 4" (10.2 cm) files are smaller in diameter than the 6" (15. 2 cm) files and are nice for getting into tiny spaces.

Sandpaper

Sandpaper is typically sold in sheets. I tear a piece about 1" (2.5 cm) square off the sheet to work with, and I pitch it when the grit has worn off and is no longer doing its job. The smaller the number grit, the more coarse the sandpaper. You can find jeweler's sandpaper grit as ultra fine as 8000! Sandpaper can be purchased from hardware stores, and from my research, the finest grit carried there is 600. Finer grits can be purchased from jewelry-supply stores.

The finest sandpaper grit I use is 330, which is still somewhat coarse, but I don't like super-polished surfaces. Instead, I like to leave some texture in my metal, leaving my creative signature.

Silver Black or Liver of Sulfur (LOS)

Silver Black is a nice product to use for darkening, or "to patina" your silver, as it has very little odor. Liver of sulfur smells like eggs, but Silver Black works just as nicely as liver of sulfur does. The process of using Silver Black is discussed in Techniques, page 21.

Tongs or Tweezers

I accidentally put a ring with a mother-of-pearl bead into Silver Black and the pearl sizzled! For that reason alone, when using Silver Black, you should use tongs or tweezers to dip and remove your jewelry from the liquid.

Steel Wool

Once you've used Silver Black on your metal, it needs to be cleaned with steel wool. Steel wool will give the metal a satin finish. The more you rub the metal with steel wool, the more Silver Black will be removed. It's not possible to remove all the Silver Black, so be sure you really want to patina the piece before doing so!

Another use for steel wool is removing tool marks. Keep in mind if you file with a metal file or sandpaper, you are changing the integrity of the metal by leaving file marks. The file marks can be sanded out with finer and finer sandpaper. Although steel wool is also changing the integrity of the metal, it does so in such a sublime manner that it's not noticeable other than the fact that it removes tool marks. It takes a bit of perseverance to get the marks out, but is always well worth the effort.

Brass Bristle Brush

When using steel wool to remove excess Silver Black or liver of sulfur, little bits and pieces will get wedged into coils and weaves. To remove these, use a brass bristle brush and gently brush the jewelry in the direction of the weave or coil. Some pieces of steel wool will have to be pulled out using your fingers or tweezers as they can really get wedged into the jewelry, but for the most part, the brass brush will work well for this task. I also hold my jewelry about 2" (5.1 cm) above my work bench and drop it a few times, which helps to remove minute fibers that the brushing misses. The brass bristle brush will not only help remove steel wool fibers, but will also help remove excess Silver Black.

Rotary Tumbler

Yes, woven jewelry can be tumbled! To add a shine or really clean up your jewelry, a rotary tumbler can be used with stainless steel shot and a small amount of burnishing liquid or soap. I like to use Dawn soap because it also acts as a degreaser.

Throughout *Weave Wrap Coil* the project instructions will refer you back to this chapter for the techniques used. If weaving and/or coiling are new to you or you need a refresher, you may want to practice the techniques first before getting started on any projects. Also, in this chapter are helpful hints on working with 26-gauge wire such as how to avoid kinks and how to weave in small spaces.

Wire Wrapping

You'll be doing some basic wire wrapping for the jewelry projects in this book, so read on to either learn how or to brush up on these techniques. I'll also show how to make a quick and easy spiral hook for bracelets and necklaces and customized ear wires. Let's start with simple loops.

Simple Loops

Learn how to make simple loops using a wire template. You can make big or small loops using this technique.

1   Flush cut 2" (61 cm) of 20-gauge dead-soft or half-hard wire.

2   Mark a spot on the top jaw of your round-nose pliers with a permanent marker about one-third of the way from the tip. (Don't worry about ruining your pliers—this mark will eventually wear off or can be rubbed off.) If your round-nose pliers jaws are black, use masking or painter's tape to mark the spot (painter's tape is usually blue, is low stick, and can be found at a hardware store).

3   Use the round-nose pliers to grasp the wire end at the mark. The tip of the wire should be as flush as possible to the pliers' jaws so that when you run your finger down the side of the jaws, the wire can either not be felt or just barely be felt.

4   Roll the pliers away from you about one-quarter turn or until your wrist is fully extended in a rolling motion. Reposition your pliers in the loop and finish rolling the wire until the flush cut end touches the wire.

5   Use the permanent marker to mark the wire where the flush cut touches the wire's neck. Add some masking tape at the mark (Figure 1).

figure 1

6   Use your round-nose pliers to unroll the loop. Use chain-nose or parallel pliers to flatten any kinks. **NOTE:** Don't use nylon-jaw pliers as they will most likely wipe off the mark.

7   Measure the length of the wire from the tape mark to the flush-cut end. My mark is ½" (1.3 cm). This tells me that to make a loop at the mark placed on my round-nose pliers, I need ½" (1.3 cm) of wire. This template can be used when making additional loops so that you know where to make your 90° bend (Step 8), or you can measure the wire to make your bend. The template is handy if you end up with an odd measurement, or you can make a new template, starting back at Step 2, with a new mark on your pliers.

8   Cut 2" (1.3 cm) of 20-gauge wire. Make a 90° bend in the wire per the length of your template (Figure 2).

figure 2

9 Use your round-nose pliers to grasp the wire end at the mark and roll until the flush cut end touches the wire at the bend. If necessary, place chain-nose pliers inside the loop against the bend and slightly tilt the wire to center the loop (Figure 3).

figure 3

Eventually you will not require a template or measuring as you will know visually where to place the pliers on the wire that is to be looped. **NOTE:** The length of wire needed to make loops will change with each gauge. For example, I may use ⅜" (9 mm) to make a loop with 20-gauge wire, but the same sized loop may require ½" (1.3 cm) with 16-gauge wire.

Opening and Closing Loops

Sometimes it's necessary to open a simple loop to coil your weaving wire within the loop. Never uncurl the loop as it will lose its shape. Instead, the loop is swung open like a door. This is also how jump rings are opened and closed. To open a loop, use chain-nose pliers to slowly bend the loop open, parallel to the frame wire. To close the loop, make the same motion in reverse.

Handmade Chain

This chain is easy to make. It's also very versatile, as the loops can be the same size, or you can vary them for a different look. To make handmade chain, you need to know how much wire you'll use to make a simple loop (see Simple Loop, page 13). Determine this measurement, then multiply that measurement by 2, as two loops are made for one chain segment. When calculating how many chain segments to make to obtain the length desired for your bracelet or necklace, remember to add in the length of the clasp.

1 Flush cut the required amount of 16-gauge wire for one chain segment.

2 Form a simple loop on one end of the wire.

3 Form a simple loop on the other wire end, rolling the loop in the opposite direction of the first loop (Figure 4).

figure 4

4 Measure the chain segment to calculate how many segments are needed for the desired length of your piece, adding the length of your clasp to the measurement of your overall length. Create enough segments to complete your piece.

5 If you plan on incorporating a hook clasp, be sure to make a chain segment with a loop large enough for the hook to fit through. For this segment, don't cut the wire from the spool, but rather make the large loop, then measure from the point at which the large loop ends and cut the length required to form the second loop (Figure 5).

figure 5

6 To attach the chain segments to one another, open a segment loop as you would a jump ring, slip on a second segment, then close the loop; repeat to connect all the segments and the clasp at the end.

Wrapped Loops

Wrapped loops take a bit more practice than simple loops, but personally, I think it's easier to make wrapped loops than it is to make simple loops. I also think wrapped loops are much more functional and secure than simple loops.

1 Cut 6" (15.2 cm) of 20-gauge dead-soft or half-hard wire. Form a 90° bend 2" (1.3 cm) from one end of the wire.

2 In order to make the loop for this technique, you need to determine two things: The spot on the pliers at which you'll be making the loop and how much wire is required for that spot. If necessary, please refer to Simple Loops, page 13.

Grasp the wire at a point halfway from the bend and the length usually required to form a simple loop. For example, when I form simple loops, I need ½" (1.3 cm) of wire to make the full loop, so I grasp the wire ¼" (6 mm) from the bend.

3 Roll your pliers away from you, until you've made one-half of the loop (Figure 6).

figure 6

4 While holding the wire in the pliers, grab the wire tail with your free hand and pull it underneath the pliers so it's perpendicular to the wire stem. As you pull the wire you may need to roll your pliers slightly again in order to not overextend or under-extend the loop. The best thing to do is to watch to make sure you don't roll or pull the bend out. **NOTE:** There's a fine line between rolling and/or pulling the bend out of the wire, but with a little practice, you will get a feel for it in no time by watching as you make the loop.

5 Use chain-nose pliers to grasp the loop just made with the wire tail facing away from you.

6 Grab the wire tail with your free hand and coil it around the wire stem three or four times (Figure 7).

7 Flush cut the wire tail close to the coil (Figure 8).

figure 7   figure 8

8 If necessary, use chain-nose pliers to gently squeeze the wire end into the coil.

Spiral Hook

This hook uses a very small amount of wire and is easy to make. I usually make ten to fifteen at a time and store them in a plastic bag so I have them readily available.

1 Flush cut 3" (7.6 cm) of 16-gauge dead-soft wire.

2 Use the large end of round-nose pliers to form a loop at one end of the wire. Continue rolling loosely so the wire follows about a quarter of the way around the loop.

3 Use nylon-jaw pliers to grasp the loop just made. Roll the wire around the initial loop until it reaches the loop's top (Figure 9). **NOTE:** This step can be done with chain- or flat-nose pliers, but nylon-jaw pliers won't mar the wire.

figure 9

4 Use the large end of round-nose pliers to grasp the straight wire at its midpoint.

5 Roll the pliers so the wire bends back toward the base loop made in Steps 2 and 3, forming the hook.

6 Use the small end of round-nose pliers to form a small loop at the other wire end, rolling the loop in the opposite direction of the first loop.

7 Use the large end of round-nose pliers to grasp the hook's center. Push the small loop toward the large one, leaving a small space between the wires (Figure 10).

figure 10

8 To attach the hook to a piece of jewelry, open the large loop as you would open a simple loop (see Opening and Closing Loops, page 14), attach the hook, and close the loop. Spiral hooks can also be attached with jump rings. To attach the hook, open the small loop made in Step 6 and the base loop made in Steps 2–3 as you would open a simple loop.

9 **OPTION:** Use a hammer and anvil to forge the arch of the hook, work-hardening the wire. File and sand the hook.

Ear Wires

I really like to make my own ear wires because I can customize them to match my earrings. Use small pieces of coil or beads to decorate the ear wires.

1 Flush cut 2" (1.3 cm) of 20-gauge half-hard wire. Use the small end of round-nose pliers to form a P-shaped loop at one end of the wire.

2 Place one small piece of coil or a 2mm, 3mm, or 4mm bead on the wire, and slide it down to the simple loop.

3 With chain-nose pliers, grab the wire about 1 mm above the coil or bead and form a 45° bend in the wire (Figure 11).

NOTE: If the bead is glass, form the bend with your thumbnail instead of chain-nose pliers to avoid the risk of cracking the bead.

figure 11

4   Hold the wire in the large end of round-nose pliers at the bend just made, with the simple loop closure pointing away from you. Grab the wire end with needle-nose pliers and pull it down and around the round-nose pliers (Figure 12).

5   Use chain-nose pliers to form a small bend at the wire end (Figure 13).

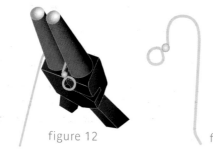

figure 12   figure 13

Wire Weaving

For the projects in this book, I'll show five types of wire-weaving techniques. Below are step-by-step instructions and illustrations of these techniques. Before I begin, some things to keep in mind:

- Keeping frame wires relatively parallel to each other is important, but they don't need to be perfectly parallel. When the frames are shaped into a bracelet, for example, it's very difficult, if not at all discernable, to see that the frames are not perfectly parallel. As you're weaving, check the frame wires frequently. If you pull your weaving wire parallel to the frames, you will most likely misalign one or both of the frame wires. I have found the best way to avoid this is to pull the weaving wire at a 90° angle, not parallel, to the frames. If your frame wires become misaligned, use chain-nose pliers to gently realign the wires back into place.

- Always pull the weaving/coiling wire snugly around the frame to help prevent the wire from bulging or buckling.

- Be sure to maintain the wire's tension while weaving. Having a tight weave will give your jewelry a beautiful uniform

appearance. Since all wire has a spring to it, it's important to push the weave together with your fingers from time to time. The wire will still spring back, but the more you push the weave together, the less the wire will move. When using my technique to end short wire and add new wire (see page 19), having a tight uniform weave will create a smooth, seamless transition and hide the wire ends.

- When weaving an angled frame, it's best to start at the narrowest point and weave to the widest point. It's difficult to weave from the widest to the narrowest point because the wire slips down the angle. For a small project such as the Diamond Pendant, page 22, or the Jules' Ring, page 66, it's possible to weave from wide to narrow because the spacing between the frame wires is close, and it's easy to hold the wire in place, keeping it from slipping. A frame that would be very difficult to weave from wide to narrow is the Autumn Leaf Bracelet, page 110.

- When you're getting started, keep in mind that it's easiest to weave near the end of the frame wires when possible, helping keep the frame wires parallel.

Weave Pattern 1

Weave Pattern 1 is made with two frame wires woven together.

1   Cut two 6" (15.2 cm) pieces of 16-gauge dead-soft wire. These are the frame wires.

2   Cut 3' (.9 m) of 26-gauge wire. This is the weaving wire.

3   Leaving 1" (2.5 cm) of tail wire to hold onto, coil the weaving wire around one of the frame wires two to three times about 1" (2.5 cm) from the frame wire's end. This is Frame Wire 1.

4   Hold the second piece of 16-gauge wire (Frame Wire 2) parallel to Frame Wire 1. Bring the weaving wire underneath and over Frame Wire 2; coil twice (Figure 14).

5   Bring the weaving wire underneath and over Frame Wire 1; coil twice (Figure 15).

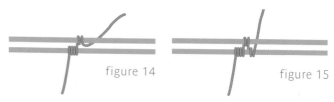

figure 14   figure 15

6   Continue weaving, repeating Steps 4–5 (Figure 16). As you near the end of the frame wires, push the weave to the left to continue weaving.

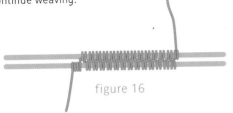

figure 16

Weave Pattern 2

Weave Pattern 2 is made with two arched wires woven together.

1   Cut two 6" (15.2 cm) pieces of 16-gauge dead-soft wire.

2   Arch the wires on a bracelet mandrel. One frame wire needs to be arched slightly smaller than the second frame wire so they fit side by side (Figure 17).

3   Cut 3' (.9 m) of 26-gauge wire. This is the weaving wire.

4   Leaving 1" (2.5 cm) of tail wire to hold onto, coil the weaving wire around the smaller frame wire two to three times about 1" (2.5 cm) from the end. This is Frame Wire 1.

5   Hold the second piece of 16-gauge wire (Frame Wire 2) parallel to Frame Wire 1. Bring the weaving wire underneath and over Frame Wire 2; coil three times (Figure 18).

6   Bring the weaving wire underneath and over Frame Wire 1; coil twice (Figure 19).

7   Continue weaving, repeating Steps 5 and 6 (Figure 20). As you near the end of the frame wires, push the weave to the left to continue weaving.

Weave Pattern 3

Weave Pattern 3 is very similar to Weave Pattern 1, it just has another piece of wire in the center.

1   Cut three 6" (15.2 cm) pieces of 16-gauge dead-soft wire. These are the frame wires.

2   Cut 3' (.9 m) of 26-gauge wire. This is the weaving wire.

3   Leaving 1" (2.5 cm) of tail wire to hold onto, coil the weaving wire around one of the frame wires two to three times about 1" (2.5 cm) from the end. This is Frame Wire 1.

4   Hold the second and third pieces of 16-gauge wire (Frame Wires 2 and 3) parallel to Frame Wire 1. Bring the weaving wire underneath Frame Wire 2 and over Frame Wire 3; coil twice (Figure 21).

5   Bring the weaving wire over Frame Wire 2, underneath and over Frame Wire 1; coil twice (Figure 22).

6   Continue weaving, repeating Steps 4 and 5 (Figure 23). As you near the end of the frame wire, push the weave to the left to continue weaving.

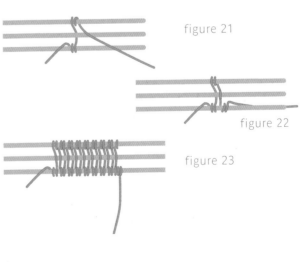

figure 21

figure 22

figure 23

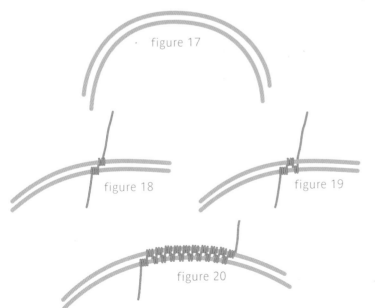

figure 17

figure 18

figure 19

figure 20

Weave Pattern 4

This pattern is similar to Weave Pattern 3 as it uses three pieces of wire. In Weave Pattern 3, the weaving wire is not woven around the center frame wire but goes under or over the wire. In this pattern, the center wire is woven.

1   Cut three 6" (15.2 cm) pieces of 16-gauge dead-soft wire. These are the frame wires.

2   Cut 3' (.9 m) of 26-gauge wire. This is the weaving wire.

3   Leaving 1" (2.5 cm) of tail wire to hold onto, coil the weaving wire around one of the frame wires two to three times about 1" (2.5 cm) from the end (Figure 24). This is Frame Wire 1.

4   Hold the second piece of 16-gauge wire (Frame Wire 2) parallel to Frame Wire 1. Bring the weaving wire underneath Frame Wire 2; coil once.

5   Bring the weaving wire over Frame Wire 3; coil twice (Figure 25).

6   Bring the weaving wire over Frame Wire 2; coil once (Figure 26).

7   Bring the weaving wire underneath Frame Wire 1; coil twice (Figure 27).

8   Continue weaving, repeating Steps 4–7 (Figure 28). As you near the end of the frame wire, push the weave to the left to continue weaving.

Weave Pattern 5

Weave Pattern 5 is a basketweave; I love the look!

1   Cut three 6" (15.2 cm) pieces of 16-gauge dead-soft wire. These are the frame wires.

2   Cut 3' (.9 m) of 26-gauge wire. This is the weaving wire.

3   Coil the weaving wire two times around a frame wire (this is Frame Wire 1). Hold a second piece of 16-gauge wire parallel to Frame Wire 1. Coil the weaving wire around both frame wires three times about 1" (2.5 cm) from the end. On the third coil, bring the weaving wire up between the two frame wires (Figure 29). **NOTE:** The coils made around the first frame wire were done to maintain space when the second frame wire was added. Uncoil the two coils of wire.

4   Hold the third piece of 16-gauge wire parallel to the two frame wires. Coil the weaving wire around the second and third frame wires three times. On the third coil, bring the weaving wire behind all three frame wires (Figure 30).

5   Coil the weaving wire around the first two frame wires three times and on the third coil, bring the weaving wire up between the two frame wires (Figure 31).

6   Coil the weaving wire around the second and third frame wires three times. On the third coil, bring the weaving wire behind all three frame wires (Figure 32).

7   Continue weaving, repeating Steps 5 and 6 (Figure 33). As you near the end of the frame wire, push the weave to the left to continue weaving.

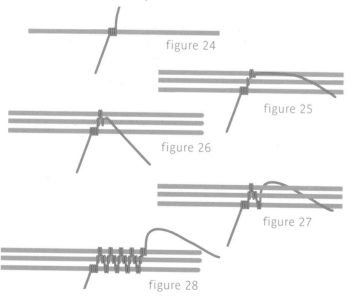

figure 24

figure 25

figure 26

figure 27

figure 28

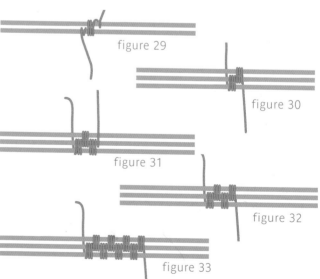

figure 29

figure 30

figure 31

figure 32

figure 33

Weaving in Small Spaces

With all the patterns I've described, you're working with pieces of wire that aren't attached to beads or wrapped around anything. In the book projects, all wires are connected to something at some point and there will be times when the space to weave gets really small, making weaving somewhat challenging.

As you pull wire through a small space, it will most likely twist into a loop, which will lead to a kink. The wire can also bend and then won't pull through the weave opening smoothly or worse yet, break at the bend. There is an easy way to fix these problems:

1   Pull the wire slowly.

2   If the wire does twist, untwist it with your fingers.

3   Continue pulling. When the loop is too small to manipulate with your fingers and if it starts to bend or twist, place the tip of a yarn needle in the loop to straighten the wire, then continue pulling until the wire is snug against the needle. Remove the needle and pull the wire the rest of the way through.

Wire Kinks

As you weave wire, a loop might form as it's being pulled through the frames. When this happens, the loop gets smaller and smaller until a kink forms. To remedy this, uncurl and straighten the wire as soon as a loop begins to form. I always uncurl the wire with my fingers, not a tool, simply because if I uncurl the loop as soon as it starts to form, it's large enough that no tool is required to undo it.

If you don't realize a loop has formed and the kink becomes small, you may need to use chain-nose pliers to unbend the kink, followed by nylon-jaw pliers to straighten the wire as best you can.

When a kink becomes really small, chances are you won't be able to get the bend mark out of the wire, which ultimately may be noticeable in your weave. I have unkinked wire only to have it break at that spot as it has been weakened significantly, so keep your wire as straight as possible when weaving!

Uncurling Wire

When pulling the weaving/coiling wire through your fingers, don't tightly squeeze the wire or run your fingernails along the wire. Both have the same effect as when you pull a scissors over a ribbon to curl it. Avoid doing this because curls and loops can turn into kinks. When pulling the wire, do so with the pads of your fingers with gentle pressure. I avoid using nylon-jaw pliers to straighten 26-gauge wire because if too much pressure is used, this can also curl the wire.

Adding Weaving Wire

Adding weaving wire is a little tricky, but with some practice, you can obtain a seamless transition. This technique works well for all the weaving patterns starting on page 16, except for Weave Pattern 5. To add weaving wire to Weave Pattern 5, see page 20.

1   End the old wire by first coiling the weaving wire once around the frame wire.

2   Trim the weaving wire tail on the inside of the frame wire (Figure 34).

3   Push the tail wire away from the woven wire, then uncoil it from the frame wire (Figure 35).

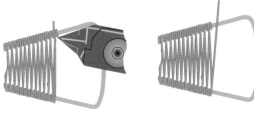

figure 34   figure 35

4   Use chain-nose pliers to grasp the end of the weaving wire and pull it to the inside of the frame wire. Doing this makes the tension on the wire very tight.

5   Trim the weaving wire tail a second time on the inside of the frame wire.

6   If necessary, use chain-nose pliers to carefully squeeze the end of the tail wire against the frame. Use your thumbnail to push the tail wire against the weave.

7   Start a new wire by first cutting the desired length of weaving wire.

8 Coil the weaving wire one time around the frame wire in the same direction you were coiling with the last piece of weaving wire (Figure 36).

figure 36

9 Following your weave pattern, weave around the next frame wire.

10 Push the new weaving wire slightly away from the weave, then cut the tail.

11 Repeat Steps 3–6, then resume your weave pattern.

Adding Weaving Wire for Weave Pattern 5

Adding weaving wire for Weave Pattern 5 is very easy!

1 After coiling around two frame wires three times, trim the weaving wire's tail on the backside of the frame wire.

2 Use your fingernail to press the weaving wire against the frame wire. **NOTE:** Chain-nose pliers will not work for this job.

3 Start a new wire by first cutting the desired length of weaving wire.

4 Thread the weaving wire between the two frame wires where the last basketweave was made.

5 Following the basketweave, coil the next set of two frame wires, then coil the next set of two frame wires.

6 Trim the new weaving wire's beginning tail and repeat Step 2.

Coiling

Coiling can be done using a mandrel or coiled directly onto frame wire. I always try to coil directly on the frame wire that I'm working on because it's time efficient, but it's not always possible. Your alternative is to use a mandrel: cut a 6" (15.2 cm) piece of copper wire the same gauge as your project, coil on this mandrel, remove the coil, and slide it onto the project wire.

When first learning how to coil, it's best to work with 2' to 3' (61 cm to .9 m) of 26-gauge wire at a time. A general rule of thumb is to cut the wire as long as your arm. As you master this skill, you'll be able to work with longer pieces.

Some intermediate and advanced projects require one long coil. When coiling 4' (1.2 m) or more, I find it best to stand while coiling so the uncoiled wire can hang to the ground and freely turn, giving it less chance to become kinked and tangled. Also keep in mind that coiling wire may form loops that turn into kinks. Uncurl and straighten the wire before a kink forms.

1 Cut 6" (15.2 cm) of 16-gauge wire and 8" to 10" (20.3 to 25.4 cm) of 26-gauge wire.

2 Hold the 26-gauge wire against the 16-gauge wire with your nondominant hand, leaving at least a 1" (2.5 cm) tail to hold onto.

3 It's easiest to coil near the end of the mandrel. Grasp the long end of the 26-gauge wire and begin rotating your hand away from your body, keeping tension on the wire, which helps create a uniform coil. Keep the coiled revolutions parallel to and touching each other. As you coil around the mandrel, let the wire in your dominant hand turn freely to avoid kinking and tangling.

4 As the coil reaches the end of the mandrel, push it toward the middle of the mandrel; resume coiling.

5 Once you've completed the coil, straighten the starting tail. Unwind the starting tail, push the wire against the coil (Figure 37), then trim.

figure 37

6 Trim the wire tails and use chain-nose pliers to gently squeeze the wire end flush against the mandrel.

7 If additional wire is needed to complete your coiling, cut a new piece of wire, leave a 1" (2.5 cm) wire tail to hold onto, and resume coiling. When you're done coiling, cut the 1" (2.5 cm) tail, squeeze the end down, then roll the coil until the new coil end matches up with the old coil end.

Forging

Hammering, or forging, wire is a technique that adds dimension to any piece of jewelry. It also strengthens, or "work-hardens" your wire, which is helpful for creating durable spiral hooks and arches.

To forge, you'll need a steel block or anvil and a goldsmith's hammer. I like to place my metal block on an old scrap of leather as it helps muffle the hammering noise.

1   Use your nondominant hand to hold the wire half on/half off a steel block or anvil, keeping your fingers off the block.

2   Use a goldsmith's hammer to lightly tap the arch of the wire. Turn the wire over and lightly hammer the other side. This can be repeated as desired, but keep in mind that the more you hammer, the thinner the wire becomes.

3   After forging, there will be hammer marks on your wire. These marks can be left alone, creating a rough look, or they can be filed and/or sanded to create a smooth look. When I want to remove my hammer marks, I start filing with a coarse metal file, then switch to fine sandpaper grit (see Filing and Sanding, below).

Filing and Sanding

Sometimes you'll find it necessary to file or sand your wire to remove tool marks. I find it easiest to place the wire on a flat surface or hold it against the index finger of my non-dominant hand, then file until the tool marks are gone. I always file the wire edge, too, to shape it nicely and smooth out any sharp or bumpy edges.

Filing with a coarse metal file will leave file lines in the metal. If you want to remove file lines, use fine sandpaper. I sand with sandpaper the same way I sand with a metal file. See page 11 for more information on sandpaper.

Antiquing or Oxidizing Silver

Liver of sulfur and Silver Black are chemicals used to patina metals. They give metal an aged, or antique look. I prefer to use Silver Black, as liver of sulfur has the very strong odor of eggs. Silver Black does have an odor but should be used in a well-ventilated area.

For this technique, you'll need Silver Black, tongs or tweezers, a towel, steel wool, and a brass bristle brush. If I'm antiquing one or two rings, I use an old coffee cup as the soaking pot; for larger pieces I use a glass bowl.

NOTE: Never place porous beads, such as mother-of-pearl or pearls, into patina chemicals. I was antiquing a group of rings one day and had a mother-of-pearl ring that I accidentally put into Silver Black with the rest of the group of rings . . . that bead went from being a pretty pearly white to a not-so-pretty gray. The pearl literally fizzled in the Silver Black!

1   Set your glass container inside a sink. Close the drain so you don't lose any pieces of jewelry.

2   Silver Black can be diluted, which makes the product last much longer. I use a 1:1 mixture with water. Just fill the Silver Black container's lid with the product and empty it into a glass container. Fill the lid with water and empty it into the same glass container. This can be repeated, depending on how many pieces of jewelry you are antiquing. One capful of Silver Black and one capful of water is the perfect amount for two rings.

3   Use the tongs to place the jewelry in the mixture until it is completely blackened.

4   Remove the jewelry with the tongs and rinse well.

5   Place the jewelry on a towel and let air-dry.

6   If there is any mixture left, pour it back into the bottle. Wash the tongs and glass container with dish soap.

7   Once the pieces are dry, use steel wool to remove any excess Silver Black and to shine the highlights of the pieces. A brass bristle brush can be used to remove minute pieces of steel wool, brushing the wire in the direction of the weave or coil. I also hold my pieces about 2" (5 cm) above a countertop and drop it multiple times; this is very effective in removing tiny fibers of steel wool.

● BEGINNER

○ INTERMEDIATE

○ ADVANCED

diamond
PENDANT

This all-wire diamond-shaped pendant is a dynamic eye-catching piece that shows the true beauty of woven-wire jewelry.

DESIGN INSPIRATION

This is a great beginning lesson. Learning the concept of form-shaping with weaving opens the door to endless design possibilities. I love this pendant and have one that I made with brass wire in my personal stash of jewelry.

PROJECT NOTES

The diamond-shaped frame wires need to fit together, so the angle of your bends and the size of your loops need to factor into this. If you're good at sketching, draw the diamond shape, then cut your wire and make the bends using your drawing as a template. I'm not good at sketching, so I used copper wire and followed Steps 1–8 to make my two frame wire templates before using sterling silver wire.

FINISHED SIZE

18¾" (47.6 cm)

MATERIALS

9½" (24.1 cm) of 16-gauge dead-soft wire

7' (2.1 m) of 26-gauge dead-soft wire

17" (43.2 cm) of commercial or handmade chain (page 14)

1 handmade 24mm Spiral Hook (page 15) or toggle clasp

4 round 6mm 16-gauge jump rings (if toggle and commercial chain are used)

TOOLS

Flush cutters

Flat-nose pliers

Round-nose pliers

Nylon-jaw wire-straightening pliers

Ruler

Low-stick tape

Permanent marking pen

TECHNIQUES USED

Wire Weaving (page 16)

Coiling (page 20)

1   Straighten and flush cut one 4½" (11.4 cm) and one 5" (12.7 cm) piece of 16-gauge wire. The shorter wire is the Inner Frame wire; the longer one is the Outer Frame wire.

2   Use the pen to mark the Inner Frame wire at 1½" (3.8 cm), 2¼" (5.7 cm) and 3".(7.6 cm).

3   Use flat-nose pliers to form a V-shaped bend at the 2¼" (5.7 cm) mark.

4   Use round-nose pliers to form a loop on each wire end. Each loop should face out from the V. Continue turning the loop one-quarter turn to form an open spiral (Figure 1).

5   Form 45° bends at the 1½" (3.8 cm) and 3" (7.6 cm) marks made in Step 2 so the loops touch each other (Figure 2). Set the Inner Frame aside.

6   Mark the Outer Frame wire at 1¼" (3.2 cm), 2½" (6.4 cm), and 3¾" (9.5 cm).

7   Use flat-nose pliers to form a V-shaped bend on the Outer Frame wire at the 2½" (6.4 cm) mark. Repeat Step 4.

8   Form 90° bends at the 1¼" (3.2 cm) and 3¾" (9.5 cm) marks.

9   Place the Inner Frame inside the Outer Frame to check the alignment and bends of your frames. Make adjustments as necessary (Figure 3).

10   Place the frame wires on a flat surface. Tape the middle of the frames together, then carefully pick up the frames and wrap the tape around the back. Tape the bottom of the frame wires together.

11   Cut 4' (1.2 m) of 26-gauge wire if you are comfortable working with that length; otherwise, cut 2' (61 cm) to 3' (91 cm) and add wire as necessary as you work. This is the weaving wire. Coil the two loops of the Inner Frame together ten to twelve times (Figure 4—red wire).

12   Coil one side of the Inner Frame three to five times, coiling to where the Outer Frame touches the Inner Frame.

13   Coil the Inner and Outer Frames together twelve to fourteen times, coiling until there's enough space between the two frames to begin weaving (Figure 4—blue wire). Reposition the tape as necessary. **NOTE:** Since only one side of the frames is attached, the second side of the frames needs to be taped together.

14   Work Weave Pattern 1, weaving to the Inner Frame's first bend (Figure 5).

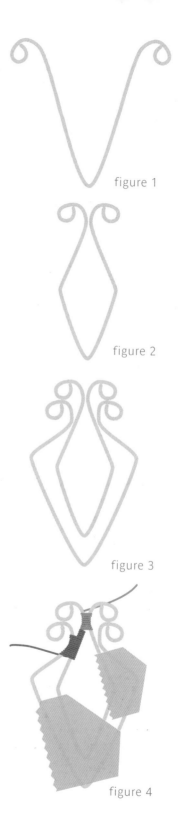

figure 1

figure 2

figure 3

figure 4

15 Coil around the bend of the Outer Frame. Count how many times you coil before getting to the center of the bend, coil one time in the center, and then coil the same number as counted. I coiled five times, one time, five times. Make note of how many times you coiled as this will be repeated on the second side of the frame.

16 Reposition the tape to the second side of the Inner and Outer Frames, making sure to line up the bottom two bends/diamond tips. Wrap the tape several times around the frame for a good hold as it's easy to pull the frames out of alignment. Check them frequently!

17 Resume Weave Pattern 1. When weaving an angled frame, the wire tends to slip down the angle. Typically it's best to weave from the narrow to the wide angle, but since the spacing between the frame wires is narrow, it's possible to weave from wide to narrow. Hold the weaving wire on the outer frame in place while weaving, pushing back to keep it tight.

18 Weave to the Inner Frame's second bend/diamond tip (Figure 6).

19 Coil around the bend of the Outer Frame. Count how many times you coil before getting to the center of the bend, coil two times in the center, and then coil the same number as counted. Cut the wire tail (Figure 7). **NOTE:** The last thing I do is cut the beginning weaving wire tail because the coiling can loosen from holding the pendant while weaving, coiling or taping/retaping. With the tail still attached, it is easy to tighten the coil back up if needed before cutting.

20 Cut 3' (.9 m) of 26-gauge weaving wire. Remove all tape. Repeat Step 12, coiling the top of the Inner Frame. Coil the same number of times as in Step 12.

21 Coil the Inner and Outer Frames together twelve to fourteen times, coiling until there's enough space between the two frames to begin weaving.

22 Repeat Steps 14–18, excluding all taping, and ending the weave on the Inner Frame.

23 Coil the inner diamond tip two to three times (Figure 8). Cut all wire tails.

24 Cut the chain in half and attach one end of each length to the diamond's upper loops. Connect the clasp to the other chain ends.

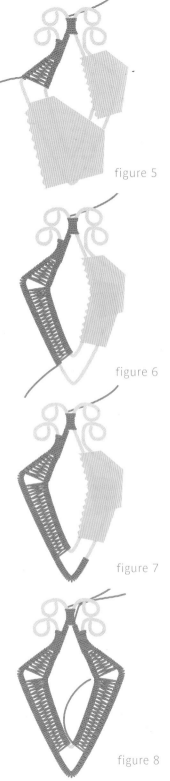

figure 5

figure 6

figure 7

figure 8

coiled
DROP EARRINGS

Green amethyst drops? Garnet drops? Top-drilled freshwater pearls? There are so many choices for these earrings, with each lending to their own unique look.

DESIGN INSPIRATION

I had a fleur-de-lis in mind when I designed these earrings. They came close to it, but maybe someday I will revisit this idea and see if I can design something a bit closer in look. I am very pleased with how these earrings turned out—simple yet sophisticated!

PROJECT NOTES

This project is a great lesson in understanding the difference between rolling and pulling your wire around round-nose pliers and mandrels. When rolling wire on round-nose pliers, the length of the wire side that is being rolled onto shortens as it becomes part of the roll/loop. When you pull wire around a mandrel or round-nose pliers, the length of the wire, on both sides remains the same because the point of the wire that held in the pliers or against a mandrel becomes part of the loop.

FINISHED SIZE
1½" (3.8 cm)

MATERIALS

2 green amethyst 10mm briolettes

9" (22.9 cm) of sterling silver 16-gauge dead-soft wire

4' (1.2 m) of sterling silver 26-gauge dead-soft wire

2 sterling silver ear wires

TOOLS

Nylon-jaw wire-straightening pliers

Flush cutters

Ruler

Permanent marking pen

Round-nose pliers

Chain-nose pliers

7 or 8mm mandrel or ballpoint pen

Silver Black or liver of sulfur and steel wool (optional)

TECHNIQUES USED

Coiling (page 20)

1   Straighten and flush cut 4½" (11.4 cm) of 16-gauge wire.

2   Use the pen to mark the wire at 2¼" (5.7 cm). Place the wide end of round-nose pliers on this mark and bend the wire in half. This is the top center loop of the earrings.

3   Measuring from the outside of the center loop, mark the wire at ⅞" (2.2 cm) (Figure 1). **NOTE:** The illustration shows the measurement taken from the outside of the wire, not the inside.

4   Hold the mandrel so it's centered on one of marks made in Step 3, and bend the wire against it to 90°. Continue to push the wire up until it touches the bend made in Step 2. Repeat this on the second mark (Figure 2).

5   Use the small end of round-nose pliers to form a simple loop on each end of the wire (Figure 3).

6   All loops should be touching. If they're not, place the round-nose pliers or mandrel into the loop and gently squeeze the wire together. If you don't use the round-nose pliers or mandrel when squeezing, the loop won't retain its round form, as wire tends to bend at the arches.

7   Repeat Steps 1–6 to form a second set of frame wires; set aside. If you don't plan on using Silver Black or liver of sulfur on your earrings, remove the ink marks with a cleaning cloth. **NOTE:** I find that when a second frame is needed for a project, it's best to make it the same time as the first for consistency in size.

8   Cut 1' (30.5 cm) of 26-gauge wire.

9   Use the 26-gauge wire to coil one of the small loops of the 16-gauge wire, passing through the small loop and the center loop (Figure 4). Coil these together four times. **NOTE:** The small loops can be opened as you would open a jump ring, making it much easier to coil.

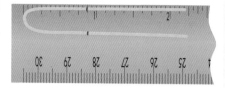

figure 1

figure 2

figure 3

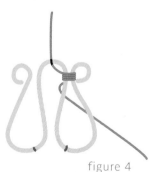

figure 4

1 0 Continue coiling around the center loop.

1 1 When you reach the second small loop, repeat Step 8.

1 2 Trim both ends of the wire and gently squeeze the ends down with chain-nose pliers (Figure 5).

1 3 Cut 1' (30.5 cm) of 26-gauge wire.

1 4 Use the new length of 26-gauge wire to coil eight times around the two wires of the center loop where the wires come together.

1 5 Continue coiling the 26-gauge wire seven times around the base of one of the loops made in Step 4 (Figure 6).

1 6 String one briolette onto the wire.

1 7 Coil the 26-gauge wire onto the base of the second loop made in Step 4, securing the briolette. Continue to coil up to the bottom of the center coil made in Step 13 until you've made seven revolutions (Figure 6).

1 8 Flush cut both wire ends and gently squeeze them down with chain-nose pliers.

1 9 Repeat Steps 7–17 to create the second earring. If desired, finish your earrings with Silver Black or liver of sulfur.

figure 5

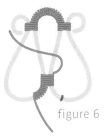

figure 6

figure 7

VARIATION

For a completely different look, use pearl instead of stone briolettes. Keep in mind that pearls shouldn't be put into Silver Black or liver of sulfur.

● **BEGINNER**
○ INTERMEDIATE
○ ADVANCED

all knotted up
RING

Fine-tune your weaving skills with this cute ring that features a tied wire knot. Once you learn how much fun it is to construct this ring, you'll soon find yourself making one for every outfit.

DESIGN INSPIRATION

I wanted to design a ring that's quick to make and thought it would be cool to come up with a ring that's tied in the center.

PROJECT NOTES

When weaving your frame wires, make sure they stay relatively parallel to each other, although they don't need to be perfectly parallel. Keep in mind that it's best to pull the weaving wire at a 90° angle to the frames. If necessary, use chain-nose pliers to gently bend the frame wire back into place.

FINISHED SIZE

Variable

MATERIALS

16" (40.6 cm) of 16-gauge dead-soft wire

10' (30.1 m) of 26-gauge dead-soft wire

TOOLS

Flush cutters

Chain-nose pliers

Nylon-jaw pliers

Ring mandrel

Metal file

Ruler

TECHNIQUES USED

Wire Weaving (page 16)

1   Straighten and cut two 8" (20.3 cm) lengths of 16-gauge wire. These are the frame wires.

2   Cut 3' (.9 m) of 26-gauge wire. This is the weaving wire.

3   Follow Weave Pattern 1 (page 16), holding the frame wires about ⅛" (3 mm) apart from each other as you weave.

4   Continue weaving and coiling, adding more weaving wire when necessary, until you've completed about 1½" (3.8 cm) of unwoven frame wire on both ends. Cut the weaving wire, leaving a 1" (2.5 cm) tail.

5   Center the woven piece on the ring mandrel at one-quarter size larger than the final desired ring size.

6   Wrap each frame end around the mandrel so they overlap each other. Use chain-nose pliers to grasp the frame wire ends and pull the frame snugly around the mandrel (Figure 1).

7   Remove the ring from the mandrel. Hold the ring with nylon-jaw pliers where the frame wires cross. Use your fingers to fold one end over the top of the ring (Figure 2).

   Continue by passing this same end through the ring shank's center (Figure 3). The weaving will spread as you bend the wires, so be sure to push the weave back.

8   If necessary, unweave the weaving wire until the frame wire shows on the inside of the ring shank. Trim the weaving wire.

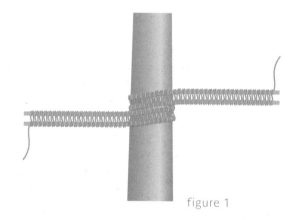

figure 1

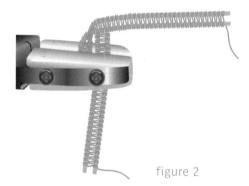

figure 2

figure 3

9 Flush cut the bent frame wire so the ends sit inside the ring. If the wire edges are sharp, file them smooth. Gently squeeze the wire ends with nylon-jaw pliers to tuck them into place inside the ring (Figure 4).

10 Place the ring on the mandrel to check its size. It should be a little smaller than when you formed the ring in Step 5 from bending the wire around the shank.

11 Remove the ring from the mandrel. Hold the ring next to the fold made in Step 7. Fold the second end over. Push the weaving back if it spreads, then pass the wires through the ring shank's center as before (Figure 5).

12 Repeat Steps 8 and 9.

13 If necessary, straighten the ring by using nylon-jaw pliers to gently squeeze along the shank.

figure 4

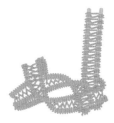

figure 5

VARIATIONS

When bending the second frame wire, don't fold it next to the first bend, but rather, leave some space between the two bends. You could even leave a small arch in the bend!

Use colorful craft wire instead of copper or silver wire.

● BEGINNER
○ INTERMEDIATE
○ ADVANCED

ocean waves
BRACELET

Imagine gentle ocean waves splashing somberly against a shoreline with all the beautiful colors of the water—greens, blues, whites—then wire-shape the waves and coil color into this beautiful bracelet.

DESIGN INSPIRATION

I was doodling with wire and this bracelet was a complete accident—the best kind of design! I was trying to make a side-by-side design where the wire came up and over the beads, but it was too unstable. As I pulled my frame wire straight, it formed this double-coiled look that really works! Adding Lori Mendenhall's beautiful swirled beads made me wish I was sitting on a beach, wearing my new bracelet.

PROJECT NOTES

We might not want to see separation in a single coil, but separation in a double coil is natural. As the single coil is being made into a double coil, the single coil "fans out." Because of the natural separation, this is a great project to practice making single coils without worrying about the separation showing.

FINISHED SIZE

8" (20.5 cm)

MATERIALS

2' (61 cm) of 18-gauge dead-soft wire

18" (45.7 cm) of 20-gauge dead-soft wire

16' (4.9 m) of 26-gauge dead-soft wire

2 swirled 18mm lentil beads

2 swirled 15 x 9mm rondelles

8 round 4mm daisy spacers

1 handmade 22mm spiral hook (page 15)

Low-stick tape

TOOLS

Flush cutters

Chain-nose pliers

Round-nose pliers

Nylon-jaw wire-straightening pliers

Bracelet mandrel

Ruler

TECHNIQUES USED

Coiling (page 20)

1   Cut 6" (15.2 cm) of 18-gauge wire to use as a coiling mandrel. Cut 18" (45.7 cm) of 18-gauge wire to use as the bracelet frame wire.

2   Cut 3' (.9 m) of 26-gauge wire and leaving a 1" (2.5 cm) wire tail, coil it onto the mandrel. Do not coil the last 1" (2. 5 cm) of wire. Remove the coil from the mandrel. Don't cut the tails.

3   Cut 6" (15.2 cm) of 20-gauge wire. Coil the 20-gauge wire around the mandrel twice. Slide the 26-gauge coil onto the 20-gauge wire and while holding onto the 26-gauge wire tail, coil this around the mandrel, creating a double coil 1" (2.5 cm) long (Figure 1).

4   Remove the double coil from the mandrel and cut all four tails. Set aside.

5   Repeat Steps 2–4 twice to form a total of three double coils.

6   Use the remaining 18" (45.7 cm) of 18-gauge wire to string 1 daisy spacer, 1 rondelle bead, 1 daisy spacer, and one coil; repeat three times, alternating the rondelle bead with a lentil bead in the second sequence. String 1 daisy spacer, 1 lentil bead, and 1 daisy spacer (Figure 2). Place low-stick tape on one side of the bracelet to keep the components from sliding off. Set aside.

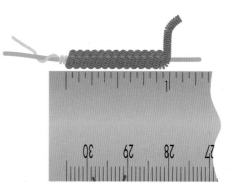

figure 1

figure 2

7   Cut 42" (1.1 m) of 26-gauge wire and coil it onto the mandrel. Remove the coil from the mandrel and cut the tails.

8   Place the coil ½" (1.3 cm) from an end daisy spacer on the 18-gauge wire. Form a 90° bend in the 18-gauge wire ¾" (1.9 cm) from the spacer (Figure 3). Be careful not to squeeze the pliers too hard, separating the coiling. **NOTE:** If the coiling becomes separated, it can be pushed back together with your thumbnail. Simply press your thumbnail between the two coils next to the separated coil on both sides.

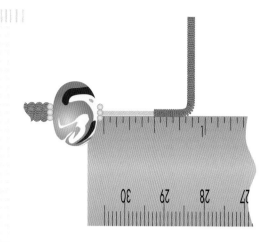

figure 3

9   Use the wide part of round-nose pliers to form a loop, again being careful to not squeeze the pliers hard (Figure 4).

10   Wrap the coiled wire up to the daisy spacer. Cut the tail.

11   Repeat Steps 7–10 on the second end of the bracelet.

12   Attach the spiral hook to one of the coiled loops.

13   Use your fingers and the bracelet mandrel to curve the coiled segments into a bracelet shape.

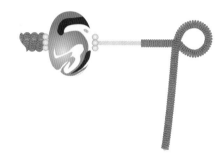

figure 4

VARIATION

The length of the bracelet can be changed by making the coiled sections shorter or longer. Another idea is to add a segment of chain to one of the end loops before wrapping it shut. Add a small bead on the end of the chain, not only because it looks nice, but also because it adds some weight to the chain. Do this by sliding a bead onto a head pin and forming a wrapped loop that attaches to the chain.

kokopelli
EARRINGS

Show off your weaving perfection with these versatile earrings. Change up the size of the loops or add bead drops to express your own twist to this beautiful design.

DESIGN INSPIRATION

When I was first designing these earrings, I had in mind to create moon-shaped earrings. After I made a couple of pairs, refining the design, it struck me that the earrings look more like a Kokopelli than a moon . . . or maybe I think that from having lived my entire life in the Southwest!

PROJECT NOTES

I find that when a second frame is needed for a project, it's best to make it the same time as the first for consistency in size. Another great little trick is to open loops that need to be coiled in as this makes coiling much easier.

FINISHED SIZE

1¾" (4.5 cm)

MATERIALS

11" (27.9 cm) of 16-gauge copper wire

6' (1.8 m) of 26-gauge copper wire

2 ear wires

2 copper 2" (5.1 cm) head pins (optional)

2 copper 4mm beads (optional)

TOOLS

Round-nose pliers

Chain-nose pliers

Flush cutters

Nylon-jaw pliers

Ring mandrel

Low-stick tape

Ruler

Permanent marker

Silver Black or liver of sulfur and steel wool (optional)

TECHNIQUES USED

Wire weaving (page 16)

Coiling (page 20)

1. Straighten and flush cut one 2½" (6.4 cm) and one 3" (7.6 cm) piece of 16-gauge wire. Use the permanent marker to mark the center of each piece. These are the frame wires.

2. Hold the center of the 3" (7.6 cm) wire on size 15 of the ring mandrel and push both ends around the mandrel, making a U shape.

3. Hold the center of the 2½" (6.4 cm) wire on size 13 of the ring mandrel and push both ends around the mandrel, making a U shape.

4. Use the large end of round-nose pliers to form a simple loop on each end of the 3" (7.6 cm) wire so they both curl outward (Figure 1).

5. Use the large end of round-nose pliers to form a simple loop on each end of the 2½" (6.4 cm) wire so they both curl inward (Figure 2).

6. Repeat Steps 1–5 to form a second set of frame wires; set aside.

7. Lay the wires next to each other on a flat surface. If the wires do not fit next to each other, reshape them on the ring mandrel (Figure 3). The loops at the top and bottom of each wire should touch.

8. With the wires on a flat surface, tape the top set of loops, carefully pick up the frame, and wrap the tape around the back of the loops.

9. Cut 3' (.9 m) of 26-gauge wire. Start coiling the wire around the bottom of the two loops (Figure 4).

figure 1

figure 2

figure 3

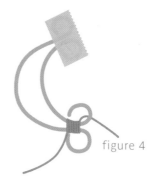
figure 4

1 0 Close the loops and form a few more coils until there is space between the two frame wires, giving you room to weave.

1 1 Follow Weave Pattern 2 (page 17) to weave the two frame wires together. Add more weaving wire as necessary and continue weaving until there isn't enough space between the frame wires to weave. Remove the tape.

1 2 Open the bottom loops, then coil the frame wires and loops together. Close the loops (Figure 5). Repeat with the top loops (Figure 6).

1 3 Trim the wire tails. Use chain-nose pliers to gently squeeze or push the ends down against the frame wire or between the two frame wires.

1 4 Attach the topmost loop to an ear wire.

1 5 Repeat Steps 7–14 to form the second earring.

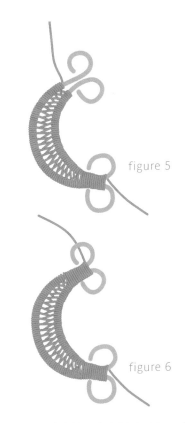

figure 5

figure 6

VARIATION

To get the look shown at right, slide a bead onto a 2" (5.1 cm) head pin, then form a wrapped loop that attaches to the upper inside loop.

Make small loops instead of large loops, then antique your earrings with Silver Black before attaching the ear wires.

● BEGINNER
○ INTERMEDIATE
○ ADVANCED

bow tie
RING

This cute coiled ring can be made up in a snap. The design is versatile since the focal bead can be featured solo, surrounded by daisy spacers, or captured between bead caps.

DESIGN INSPIRATION

I got the idea for this ring when looking at the line of rings made by Jeffrey Appling of Rings That Rock. His ring shanks feature two hands holding the stones in place. I have had the pleasure of meeting Jeffrey, and his design aesthetic is amazing.

PROJECT NOTES

Good bead choices for this ring are 4mm, 6mm and 8mm round, bicone, rondelle, or coin-shaped beads. Keep in mind as you choose beads, too, that the 26-gauge wire needs to be able to fit through the bead hole twice.

FINISHED SIZE

6½" (16.5 cm)

MATERIALS

5" (12.7 cm) of 16-gauge dead-soft wire

4' (1.2 m) of 26-gauge dead-soft wire

1 round 6mm bead

TOOLS

Flush cutters

Nylon-jaw wire-straightening pliers

Round-nose pliers

Ruler

Ring mandrel

TECHNIQUES USED

Coiling (page 20)

1   Straighten and flush cut the 16-gauge wire. This is the frame wire.

2   Form a simple loop (page 13) on one end of the frame wire, leaving it slightly open for coiling in a later step. **NOTE:** You'll make another loop in Step 10 this same size, so take note of how much wire you used to make this one.

3   Hold the wire against the mandrel at a size one-quarter larger than the desired finished size.

4   Shape the wire around the mandrel, leaving a gap to accommodate your bead. Holding the wire against the mandrel to retain its shape, curve the wire end out with your thumb (Figure 1).

5   Use about 6" (15.2 cm) of 26-gauge wire to temporarily coil the small loop two to three times. String the bead onto the 26-gauge wire, then coil two to three times around the curved part of the frame wire (Figure 2).

6   Resize the ring shank by pulling on the curved part of the frame wire at a position on the mandrel that's one-quarter size larger than the desired finished size.

7   Remove the ring from the mandrel. Remove the bead and temporary coil.

8   Place the frame on top of a ruler, with the bottom of the small loop on the ruler's edge. Use the pen to mark the curved wire to correspond with the bottom of the small loop (Figure 3).

9   Carefully straighten the curved end of the frame wire. The best way to do this and retain the shape of your ring shank is to use nylon-jaw pliers to squeeze along the curve. Do not pull the frame wire through the straightening pliers, or you will distort the ring shank.

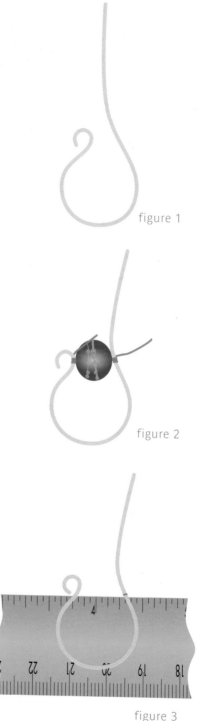

figure 1

figure 2

figure 3

1 0 Measure and flush cut the wire as needed from the mark made in Step 8; form a second simple loop. Reshape the ring shank so it's one-quarter size larger than the desired final size (Figure 4).

1 1 Cut 4' (1.2 m) of 26-gauge wire.

1 2 Leaving an 18" (45.7 cm) tail, use the 26-gauge wire to coil from the center of the ring shank to the center of the small loop.

1 3 Use the wire tail to repeat Step 12 on the second half of the ring shank (Figure 5).

1 4 String each wire tail through the bead so the wires criss-cross each other (Figure 6).

1 5 Pull each wire tail until the bead fits between the two frame wire loops.

1 6 Coil the frame wire loop with the wire tail. Cut the wire tail to the inside of the loop. Repeat to secure the wire on the second side of the ring (Figure 7).

VARIATION
Add bead caps or daisy spacers to each side of the focal bead.

figure 4

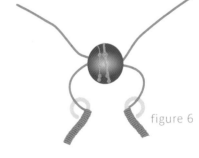

figure 5

figure 6

figure 7

● BEGINNER
○ INTERMEDIATE
○ ADVANCED

basketweave
CUFF

This cuff is elegant and rich, even though it features the simple basketweave. The design is just calling to be made in a multitude of different colors.

DESIGN INSPIRATION

I love the look of basketweave and was thrilled when I came up with this cuff. Its design warrants compliments whenever I wear it.

PROJECT NOTES

To figure how much 16-gauge wire you'll need for this project, first determine the necessary cuff length. Secondly, determine how much wire you use to make a simple loop (see page 13) and add that measurement to the cuff length. For example, I'm making a 6½" (16.5 cm) long cuff and to make two simple loops I use 1" (2.5 cm) of wire, so 6½" (16.5 cm) + 1" (2.5 cm) = 7½" (19.1 cm).

FINISHED SIZE

6½" (16.5 cm)

MATERIALS

22" to 25" (55.9 to 63.5 cm) of 16-gauge dead-soft wire (length depends on the cuff size; see Project Notes at left)

11' to 13' (3.4 to 4.6 m) of 26-gauge dead-soft wire

TOOLS

Flush cutters

Chain-nose pliers

Nylon-jaw wire-straightening pliers

Ruler

Low-stick tape

Bracelet mandrel or nylon-jaw bracelet-forming pliers

TECHNIQUES USED

Wire Weaving (page 16)

1   Straighten and flush cut three pieces of 16-gauge wire as determined in the Project Notes on page 47. These are the frame wires.

2   Form simple loops on each frame wire end so that each loop is rolled in a different direction. The loops will sit on opposite sides of the wire (Figure 1).

3   Cut 3' to 5' (.9 to 1.5 m) of 26-gauge wire or whatever length with which you're comfortable working. This is the weaving wire.

4   Coil the weaving wire two times around a frame wire (Frame Wire 1), leaving an 18" (45.7 cm) tail. Hold a second frame wire (Frame Wire 2) parallel to the first frame wire. Coil the weaving wire around both frame wires three times, coiling to the right of the loop on Frame Wire 2. On the third coil, bring the weaving wire up between the two frame wires (Figure 2). **NOTE:** It's okay if your loops overlap each other; the three frame wires are flared out in Steps 7–9.

5   Hold the third frame wire (Frame Wire 3) parallel to Frame Wires 1 and 2. Coil the weaving wire around Frame Wires 2 and 3 three times, coiling to the right of the loop on Frame Wire 3. Move the weaving so it sits against the loop on Frame Wire 3 (Figure 3). **NOTE:** The three looped frame wire ends will be woven together with the 18" (45.7 cm) wire tail in a later step.

6   Follow Weave Pattern 5 (page 18), weaving the length of the cuff to the base of the loop on Frame Wire 1 (Figure 4). Your last basketweave can be around either set of wires; you just want to be sure that the weave goes up to the base of the loop on Frame Wire 1. Add additional weaving wire as necessary (see Adding Weaving Wire: Weave Pattern 5, page 20).

figure 1

figure 2

figure 3

figure 4

7   Use chain-nose pliers to separate the three frame wires. Insert the end of the pliers between Frame Wires 2 and 3, then slide the pliers toward the weave (Figure 5). This can also be done by hand—just gently pull the frame wire ends apart.

8   Repeat Step 7 between Frame Wires 2 and 1. If necessary, slide the pliers between Frame Wires 2 and 3 again.

9   Repeat Steps 7 and 8, separating the frame wire loops on the other end of the cuff.

10 Follow Weave Pattern 3 (see page 17) to the loop curve of Frame Wire 1, weaving all three frame wire ends together. Follow Weave Pattern 1 to the loop curve of Frame Wire 2, weaving two frame wire ends together. Then coil to the loop curve of Frame Wire 3. Cut the 26-gauge wire tail on the inside of the loop (Figure 6).

11 Remove the beginning coil from Step 4 and repeat Step 10 at the other end of the cuff.

12 Shape the woven frame wires on a bracelet mandrel or with nylon-jaw bracelet-forming pliers.

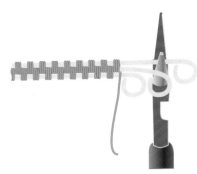

figure 5

figure 6

VARIATION

Forge and sand the loops after forming them in Step 2.

Use contrasting craft wire to make your cuff. I used copper and fuchsia in the version at right.

● BEGINNER

○ INTERMEDIATE

○ ADVANCED

caesar's scrolls
BRACELET

The beauty of swirled wire coiled together creates this regal-looking bracelet, fit for any queen to wear. This is a great project for practicing consistent looping.

DESIGN INSPIRATION

I was watching TV, doodling with wire, when I came up with this design. I wasn't sure what to name the bracelet, and when I showed it to my sister Misti she immediately said "Caesar's Scrolls." Perfect! This project can be made as earrings or a pendant, too.

PROJECT NOTES

Add coiling wire as needed throughout this project. It's best to end and start wires where two scrolls or a scroll/loop are being coiled together, as it's easier to tuck the ends in. To end a wire, cut the ending wire's tail, press it down against the frame with chain-nose pliers or your fingernail, then coil the new wire. Don't cut the new wire's tail until you coil a new section of two scrolls or a scroll/loop together or the wire may spin and pull off.

FINISHED SIZE

7" (17.8 cm)

MATERIALS

2' 6" (76 cm) to 3' (90 cm) of 16-gauge dead-soft wire

5' (1.5 m) to 7' (2.1 m) of 26-gauge dead-soft wire

2 round 8mm 16-gauge jump rings

5½" (14 cm) handmade chain (page 14)

1 handmade 22mm Spiral Hook clasp (page 15)

TOOLS

Flush cutters

Round-nose pliers

Chain-nose pliers

Nylon-jaw wire-straightening pliers

Ruler

Bracelet mandrel

TECHNIQUES USED

Coiling (page 20)

1. Straighten and flush cut 2" (5.1 cm) of 16-gauge wire.

2. Use the tip of round-nose pliers to form a loop. Continue to turn the loop one-quarter turn to form an open spiral. **NOTE:** Some of the loops will be coiled, so leave all the loops slightly open.

3. Repeat Step 2 on the second end of the wire so the loop turns in the opposite direction (Figure 1).

4. Repeat Steps 1–3 to form eleven scrolls or enough to reach 3½" (8.9 cm). **NOTE:** Use the scroll from Step 3 as a template for making the remaining scrolls; it's important that the scrolls are as close in size as possible.

5. Lay the scrolls next to one another along the edge of a ruler so each coil sits at an angle and the bottoms are aligned (Figure 2). Tape the bottoms of the scrolls together. Use another piece of tape to connect the tops of all but the first two scrolls (Figure 3).

6. Turn the scrolls over and fold the tape over to tape the back.

7. Add a small piece of tape to the middle of the first two scrolls to better stabilize the wire; the more stable the wire, the easier it will be to work with.

8. Cut 3' (.9 m) of 26-gauge wire. Coil the small loop of the second scroll to the body of the first scroll (Figure 4).

9. Coil the small loop up to where the two small loops of the scrolls touch.

10. Coil the two small loops together.

11. Remove or add tape as necessary. Coil the individual scroll up to where it touches the next scroll.

12. Coil the two scrolls together.

figure 1

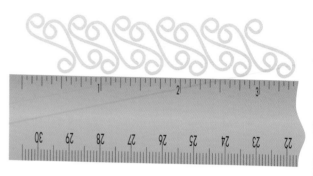

figure 2

figure 3

figure 4

13 Remove or add tape as necessary. Coil the individual scroll up to where it touches the previous scroll, then coil these scrolls together (Figure 5).

14 Remove or add tape as necessary. Coil the individual scroll up to where its small loop touches the small loop of the next scroll, then coil these loops together.

15 Remove or add tape as necessary. Coil the small loop up to where it touches the next scroll, then coil the loop and scroll together (Figure 6).

16 Remove or add tape as necessary. Coil the individual scroll up to where it touches the next scroll's small loop, then coil the scroll and loop together (Figure 7).

17 Repeat Steps 9–16 until the scrolls are completely coiled.

18 When all of the scrolls are coiled together, check to make sure any 26-gauge wire tails have been tucked in and cut.

19 Manipulate the handmade chain to form two 1¼" and two 1½" lengths. Attach a short chain to the upper loop of the first scroll, then attach a long chain to the lower loop; repeat for the second side. **NOTE:** You may need to form some of the chain links so they can fit through the scrolls at each end. The chain lengths should be even on each side, so it may be necessary to form some of the links with different-sized loops to equalize the lengths.

20 Use a jump ring to connect the end links of the short and long chains at one end of the bracelet. Use a jump ring to connect the spiral hook and the short and long chains at the other end of the bracelet (Figure 8).

21 Shape the coiled scrolls on a bracelet mandrel.

figure 5

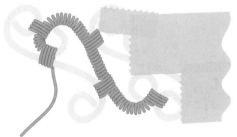

figure 6

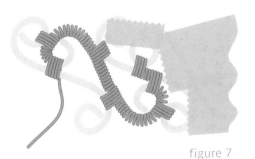

figure 7

figure 8

● BEGINNER
○ INTERMEDIATE
○ ADVANCED

swan
EARRINGS

The graceful line of a swan's neck lends to the elegant lines of this pair of earrings. Create your earrings with a longer "neck" for an even more graceful look.

DESIGN INSPIRATION

I designed an interchangeable bail for my friend Judy Payne of JP Designs for her Cool Earthwear reversible pendants. I named it the Swan Bail because they look so graceful, and one day it dawned on me that they would make cute earrings, too.

PROJECT NOTES

When you're making identical frame wires for a project, it's best to make them at the same time because you're more likely to repeat exactly what you did, such as looping your wire on the exact same spot on your round-nose pliers.

FINISHED SIZE

1⅝" (4.1 cm)

MATERIALS

8" (20.3 cm) of 16-gauge dead-soft wire

9' (2.7 m) of 26-gauge dead-soft wire

2 round 8mm jump rings

2 ear wires

TOOLS

Round-nose pliers

Flush cutters

Nylon-jaw wire-straightening pliers

Ruler

TECHNIQUES USED

Wire Weaving (page 16)

1 Straighten and cut two 4" (10.2 cm) pieces of 16-gauge dead-soft wire. These are the frame wires.

2 Use the tips of round-nose pliers to form a loop on one end of a frame wire.

3 Use the widest part of round-nose pliers to grasp the frame wire under the small loop with the loop facing you. Roll the wire until it touches the small loop (Figure 1).

4 Repeat Steps 2–3 on the second frame wire.

5 Hold one of the frame wires so the looped end made in Steps 2–3 faces to the right. Use the tips of round-nose pliers to form a loop at the other wire end that's perpendicular to the first loop. Continue to loop around about one-quarter turn, creating an open spiral (Figure 2). Set aside.

6 Repeat Step 5 with the second frame wire, but hold the wire so the looped end made in Steps 2–3 faces to the left (Figure 3).

7 Cut 4½' (1.4 m) of 26-gauge dead-soft wire. Coil one frame wire two times. Hold the second frame wire about ⅛" (3 mm) away from the first frame wire, then weave around the second frame wire following Weave Pattern 1. **NOTE:** Be sure to check the alignment of your frame wires frequently to make sure you're holding them parallel to each other.

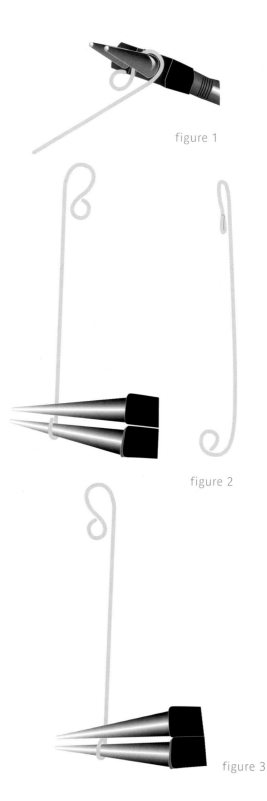

figure 1

figure 2

figure 3

8   Continue weaving, pushing the weave down the wires as necessary, until the frame wires are woven from the open spirals made in Steps 5–6 to the base of the loops made in Steps 2–4 (Figure 4). Cut the beginning weaving wire tail.

9   The two large loops can be left together or flared out. To flare the loops out, stick the barrels of round-nose pliers in the large loops, then slowly open the pliers, separating the frame wires, or flare the loops out by carefully pulling them apart with your fingers (Figure 5).

10 Continue weaving the two frame wires together, up to the curve of the large loops. Trim the weaving wire (Figure 6).

11 Repeat Steps 1–10 for the second earring. After you flare the second earring and before weaving it, hold it over the first earring to check that the frame wires are flared out the same width.

12 Hold the weaving against a ring mandrel at size 2, just underneath the large loops, and use your fingers to shape it around the mandrel. Avoid pushing the large loops around the mandrel; instead, push the small looped end around the mandrel (Figure 7). **NOTE:** The two small loops need to be at the same height level and as close as possible to the large loops so the earring hangs properly. Remove the earring from the mandrel and squeeze the loops together to get them closer. Repeat for the second earring.

13 Use a jump ring to connect each earring to an ear wire, making the attachment to the curve (not the loops) on the back frame wires.

figure 4

figure 5

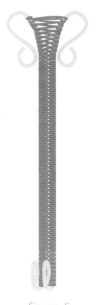

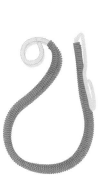

figure 6   figure 7

○ BEGINNER

● INTERMEDIATE

○ ADVANCED

sublime dreams
BRACELET

This beautiful bracelet features swirling, twisting coils that outline the stars of the show, a handful of unique lampworked beads.

DESIGN INSPIRATION

The inspiration for this bracelet came from my friend, Eni Oken. She makes a stunning advanced coiled bracelet that is much more in-depth. I wanted to make something that was not so involved, and I came up with this design. Becky of Becklin Beads created these beautiful lampworked beads.

PROJECT NOTES

You need to do some math to reach the proper length for your bracelet. Coiling adds ⅛" (3 mm) between each bead. Lay your beads out, measure the length of the beads, and add in ⅛" (3 mm) for all but one bead. With the beads I selected, plus the ⅛" (3 mm) added between all but one bead, my bracelet measures 6" (15.2 cm). Then there's a wrapped loop on each end of the bracelet, which adds another ½" (1.3 cm), plus the spiral hook, which adds another ¾" (1.9 cm). So, all together I ended up with a 7¼" (18.4 cm) bracelet.

When selecting your beads, be sure to choose a type that has bead holes large enough to accommodate 16-gauge wire.

FINISHED SIZE

7¼" (18.4 cm)

MATERIALS

5 Thai silver 12mm hexagon beads

2 turquoise/white/brown/bronze 8mm lampworked rondelle beads

2 turquoise/white/brown/bronze 16mm lampworked round beads

13" (33 cm) of sterling silver 16-gauge dead-soft wire

3' (.9 m) of sterling silver 20-gauge dead-soft wire

20' (6.1 cm) of sterling silver 26-gauge dead-soft wire

TOOLS

Nylon-jaw wire-straightening pliers

Flush cutters

Chain-nose pliers

Round-nose pliers

Bracelet mandrel (optional)

Silver Black or liver of sulfur and steel wool (optional)

TECHNIQUES USED

Coiling (page 20)

Spiral hook (page 15)

1 Straighten and cut 10" (3.1 m) of 16-gauge dead-soft wire. Form a large wrapped loop on one end of the wire. Shape the loop so it's large enough for the spiral hook to hook through.

2 String the beads onto the wire.

3 Form a small wrapped loop at the spot on the wire that would make your bracelet the length without the hook (refer to the calculation as determined in the Project Notes, page 59) (Figure 1). The bare frame wire will be covered with a coil between the beads.

figure 1

4 Cut 3' (.9 m) of 20-gauge wire; set aside. Cut 3' to 4' (.9 to 1.2 m) of 26-gauge wire.

5 Use the cut 26-gauge wire to coil onto one end of the 20-gauge wire, leaving a 1" (2.5 cm) tail.

figure 2

6 Wrap the uncoiled end of the 20-gauge wire once around the wrapped loop made in Step 1, leaving a 1" (2.5 cm) tail (the tail is created so you have something to hold onto). Push the coil all the way up against the wrap (Figure 2).

7 Wrap the 26-gauge wire's tail around the wrapped loop made in Step 1 two or three times. Cut the 26-gauge wire tail only.

8 Push and hold a bead up against the coiled 20-gauge wire, pull the coiled wire around the bead, then wrap the wire one time around the 16-gauge wire (Figure 3).

figure 3

9 Repeat Step 8 until all but the last bead is coiled and wrapped. Cut 3' to 4' (.9 to 1.2 m) lengths of 26-gauge wire and coil it onto the 20-gauge wire as needed. **NOTE:** Don't worry if the coiling doesn't lay flat. You'll be able to correct that in Step 16.

10 Once you reach the last bead, wrap one time around the wrapped loop made in Step 3 (Figure 4).

figure 4

11 Pull the 20-gauge coiled wire around the next bead and wrap one time over the previous coiled wrap made on the first half of the bracelet (Figure 5).

figure 5

1 2 Repeat Step 11 until all but the last bead is coiled and wrapped. Trim the beginning 20-gauge tail from Step 6, then wrap the coiled 20-gauge wire one time around the loop made in Step 1.

1 3 Cut the 26-gauge and 20-gauge wire tails.

1 4 Use chain-nose pliers to bend the end of the 20-gauge wire. Tuck it down against the 16-gauge frame or into the loop space (Figure 6).

1 5 Use nylon-jaw pliers to gently squeeze the coiling/wrapping in between each bead so the coiling lies flat (Figure 7).

1 6 Attach the spiral hook, then form the bracelet on a mandrel or your wrist.

figure 6

figure 7

LENGTHENING THE BRACELET

Want to lengthen your bracelet? Add a small piece of chain with a jump ring. It's also a good idea to add a small bead on the end of the chain, not only because it looks nice but because it also adds some weight to the chain. To do this, simply slide a bead onto a head pin and form a wrapped loop, attaching it to the chain before closing the loop.

BEGINNER
● INTERMEDIATE
ADVANCED

coiled heart
NECKLACE

Create this pretty coiled heart and garnet necklace with spiraled coils of garnets incorporated into the necklace chain, complementing the heart centerpiece.

DESIGN INSPIRATION

I made this heart necklace to enter in a 2009 Valentine's Day contest, but never entered it. I set it aside thinking "I'll take pictures and post it later" and then forgot to do it. Well, at least I got a cute necklace out of the deal!

PROJECT NOTES

As with Melonia's Cross (page 120), shaping your heart may take a few practice runs. Try shaping your heart first with craft, brass, or copper wire before using sterling silver.

FINISHED SIZE

19" (48.3 cm)

MATERIALS

3½" (8.9 cm) of 16-gauge dead-soft wire

20" (50.8 cm) of 20-gauge dead-soft wire

13.5' (4.1 m) of 26-gauge dead-soft wire

4 round 6mm garnets

1 freshwater 4mm pearl briolette

1 round 8mm garnet

1 metal 2" (5.1 cm) head pin

14" (35.6 cm) chain

1 heart-shaped 15mm toggle clasp

2 round 7mm 16-gauge jump rings

TOOLS

Flush cutters

Round-nose pliers

Chain-nose pliers

Flat-nose pliers

Ruler

Permanent marking pen

Nylon-jaw wire-straightening pliers

TECHNIQUES USED

Coiling (page 20)

Wrapped loop (page 14)

1   Straighten and flush cut the 16-gauge wire. This is the frame wire. Use the pen to mark the center of the wire at 1¾" (4.5 cm).

2   Use flat-nose pliers to form a bend at the mark made in Step 1, creating a V shape.

3   Use round-nose pliers to form a loop on one end of the frame wire, facing in toward the V. Leave the loop slightly open.

4   Continue looping around, creating an open spiral.

5   Repeat Steps 3–4 on the other wire end.

6   Squeeze the V together until the two loops touch (Figure 1).

7   Cut 3½' (1.1 m) of 26-gauge wire. Leaving a 4" (10.2 cm) tail, coil the two small loops together (Figure 2—red wire). Position the wire tail at the bottom of the two small loops with the long end of the 26-gauge wire at the top of the two small loops.

8   Coil the tail around a small loop three or four times, then string the pearl briolette (Figure 2—blue wire).

9   Use the same wire to coil around the second small loop, securing the briolette. Coil up to the bottom of the center coil made in Step 7, coiling three or four times to equal the coils in Step 8 (Figure 2—dark gray wire). Trim the wire tail and gently squeeze the end down with chain-nose pliers.

1 0   Use the remaining 26-gauge wire to coil around the entire heart frame. Trim the wire tail at the top of the coil made in Step 7, then gently squeeze the end down with chain-nose pliers (Figure 3).

1 1   Separate the chain into two 7" (17.8) pieces. Set aside.

1 2   Straighten and cut 10" (25.4 cm) of 20-gauge wire. Mark the wire at 4" (10.2 cm) and form a 90° bend at the mark.

1 3   Cut 2½' (76.2 cm) of 26-gauge wire and coil 3" (7.6 cm) of the 4" (10.2 cm) section of 20-gauge wire, with the coil butted up against the bend. Trim the coil's beginning tail. Don't cut the ending tail yet. **NOTE:** Leave the 26-gauge wire tail on in case you need to coil more of the 20-gauge wire in later steps.

1 4   Form a wrapped loop with the coiled section that connects to the heart frame (Figure 4). **NOTE:** When making the loop, take care to not squeeze the round-nose pliers tightly or it will separate the coiling. If the coiling separates, use your fingernail to push it back together.

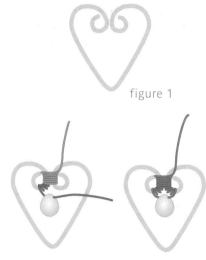

figure 1

figure 2

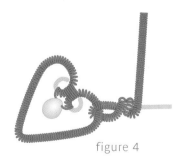

figure 3

figure 4

15 Slide a 6mm garnet onto the uncoiled section of the 20-gauge wire. If necessary for length, coil more of the 26-gauge wire tail around the uncoiled section of the 20-gauge wire, then with the coiled end of the 20-gauge wire, pull the wire down the side of the garnet. Wrap the coiled wire three times around the uncoiled 20-gauge wire. Trim the 20-gauge coiled wire tail (Figure 5).

figure 5

16 Slide a 6mm garnet onto the 20-gauge wire with the bead against the coiled section. Make a 90° bend in the 20-gauge wire, leaving enough space for another coiled wrapped loop (Figure 6).

17 Cut 2½' (76.2 cm) of 26-gauge wire and coil 3" (7.6 cm) of the 20-gauge wire, with the coil against the bend made in Step 16. Trim the beginning tail of the coil. Don't cut the ending tail yet.

figure 6

18 Form a wrapped loop that attaches to one end of a chain segment (Figure 7).

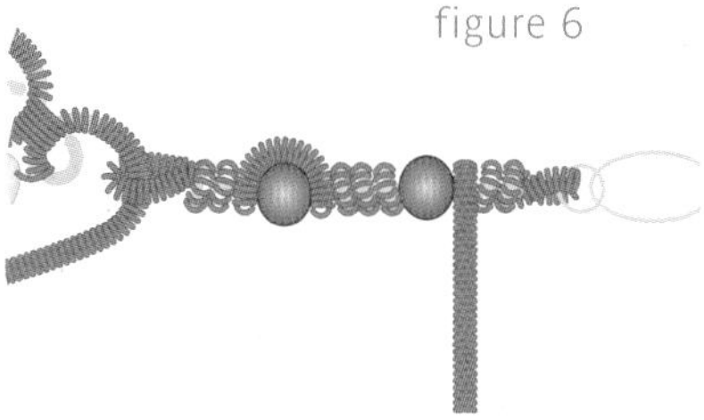

19 If necessary for length, coil more of the 26-gauge wire tail around the uncoiled section of the 20-gauge wire. Pull the coiled 20-gauge wire down the side of the closest garnet and wrap it three times around the previously wrapped/coiled segment made in Step 16 (Figure 8).

figure 7

20 To finish the wire end, it's much easier to squeeze the 20-gauge wire end down if it's not coiled. If necessary, uncoil the 20-gauge wire, then trim both the 26- and 20-gauge wire tails. Gently squeeze the wire end down.

21 Repeat Steps 12–20 to form a second coiled/beaded segment, attaching to the other side of the heart pendant. Set aside.

figure 8

22 Slide an 8mm garnet onto the head pin. Form a wrapped loop that attaches to the bottom point of the heart pendant (Figure 9).

23 Use jump rings to connect the chain ends to the clasp.

figure 9

jules'
RING

This bold ring features a vintage-style metal bead with jet rhinestones. The coiling frames the bead nicely, and the wide weaving at the back of the ring makes it extra comfortable.

DESIGN INSPIRATION

This ring is similar in technique to the All Coiled Up Ring (page 70), but this one is definitely a step up in difficulty. My little girl is not much for pink, purple, frilly or girly things, so I was surprised that she wanted one of these rings for her personal collection—I was happy to oblige and whipped up a ring for her—plus it put a big smile on my face!

PROJECT NOTES

Weaving in small openings can be a bit tricky. This is especially true with this ring, when weaving is nearly complete (Step 17). Be sure to review Weaving in Small Spaces (page 19) to prevent breaking or kinking your weaving wire.

FINISHED SIZE

25 x 18 mm (ring top)

MATERIALS

18" (45.7 cm) of 18-gauge dead-soft wire

6' (1.8 m) of 26-gauge dead-soft wire

1 two-hole 14mm bead

TOOLS

Flush cutters

Chain-nose pliers

Nylon-jaw wire-straightening pliers

Ring mandrel

File

Ruler

Yarn needle (optional)

TECHNIQUES USED

Wire Weaving (page 16)

Coiling (page 20)

1 Straighten the 18-gauge wire. String the wire through one bead hole.

2 String the other wire end through the second bead hole (Figure 1).

3 Pull one end of the wire, then the other, keeping the length of both wire ends as equal as possible. Place the ring on the mandrel at one size larger than you want your final ring size to be and continue to pull one end of the wire, then the other (Figure 2).

4 Wrap both wire ends one more time around the mandrel (Figure 3).

figure 1

5 Cut 2' (61 cm) of 26-gauge wire and coil one end of the 18-gauge wire. Push the coil to one side of the bead.

6 Wrap the beginning tail of the coil around the ring shank (Figure 4).

7 Repeat Steps 5 and 6 on the second end of the 18-gauge wire. Cut the four tails of the 26-gauge wire.

figure 2

8 Pull each coiled 18-gauge wire around the bead.

9 Wrap one end of the coiled 18-gauge wire around the ring shank one time and then place the ring on the mandrel and pull the wire end tightly (Figure 5). **NOTE:** Sometimes the shank wires in the back of the ring cross when wrapping and pulling. If necessary, use nylon-jaw pliers to gently squeeze the wires starting in the center of the shank and working toward the bead, which will uncross them.

figure 3

10 Remove the ring from the mandrel and repeat Step 9, wrapping the second wire end once around the shank.

figure 4

figure 5

1 1 Wrap the first wire end around the shank one time, check the ring size, and pull the wire. Repeat this one or two more times (Figure 6).

1 2 Repeat Step 11 for the second wire end.

1 3 Trim the 18-gauge wire ends on the inside of the ring shank. If the edges are sharp, file them smooth, then gently squeeze the wire ends with nylon-jaw pliers.

1 4 Use chain-nose pliers to separate the three 18-gauge shank wires or gently separate them with your fingers.

1 5 Cut 3' (.9 m) of 26-gauge wire.

1 6 Coil eight to ten times around the ring shank, near the wrap made in Step 11 (Figure 7).

1 7 Work Weave Pattern 3 in and out the three wires. When the space between the three wires is too narrow to weave, coil around the ring shank as was done in Step 16 (Figure 8).

1 8 Trim both tails of the 26-gauge wire and squeeze the ends down with chain-nose pliers.

figure 6

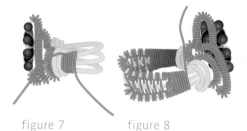

figure 7   figure 8

VARIATIONS

Instead of using Weave Pattern 3, you could use Weave Pattern 4, basketweave, for the back of the ring as shown in the photo, near right.

Darken the ring with Silver Black or liver of sulfur for an antique look, as in the photo at far right.

Also note that the 18-gauge wire is left bare at the front of the ring. To do this, simply skip Steps 5–7.

BEGINNER

● INTERMEDIATE

ADVANCED

all coiled up
RING

Frame your favorite bead with coils, add in bead caps or daisy spacers, and consider antiquing your wire to create a unique-looking, conversation-invoking ring.

DESIGN INSPIRATION

I thought adding bead caps to a ring would be something fun to experiment with, not to mention the fact that I am a complete ring junkie, so any idea for a ring is a good idea!

PROJECT NOTES

This ring is a great way to fine-tune coiling skills with consistent, even coils. If your coil becomes separated, use your fingernail to push the coils together and then make another ring for more practice.

FINISHED SIZE

18¾" (47.6 cm)

MATERIALS

12" (30.5 cm) of 18-gauge dead-soft wire

6' (1.8 m) of 26-gauge dead-soft wire

1 round 8mm to 12mm bead

2 bead caps to fit beads

TOOLS

Flush cutters

Chain-nose pliers

Nylon-jaw wire-straightening pliers

Ring mandrel

File

Ruler

Permanent marking pen

TECHNIQUES USED

Coiling (page 20)

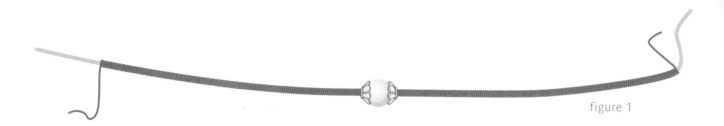

figure 1

1   Straighten the 18-gauge wire. Use the pen to mark the center of the wire.

2   Cut 3' (.9 m) of 26-gauge wire and coil it onto the 18-gauge wire. Start the coil about ½" (1.3 cm) from the pen mark. Do not coil the last 2" (5.1 cm) of the 18-gauge wire. Trim the 26-gauge wire tail near the pen mark; don't cut the second tail yet.

3   Use the 18-gauge wire to string 1 bead cap, the bead, and 1 bead cap.

4   Repeat Step 2, coiling on the second half of the 18-gauge wire (Figure 1).

5   Center the bead on the ring mandrel one size smaller than the desired final ring size. **NOTE:** You'll size it smaller here because all wire is springy, but coiled 18-gauge wire "springs back" more than normal.
    Pull one end of the 18-gauge wire around the mandrel, making a full loop around the mandrel (Figure 2).

6   Remove the ring from the mandrel, turn it over, and place it back on the mandrel. Repeat Step 5 (Figure 3).

7   Slide the ring down to the final ring size. Pull the 18-gauge wire around and down the side of the bead. Remove the ring from the mandrel, turn it over, place it back onto the mandrel, and pull the second wire around and down the side of the bead (Figure 4).

figure 2

figure 3

figure 4

8 Remove the ring from the mandrel. If the coils moved while shaping the ring, push them back toward the bead, making the coil snug and uniform. Trim the 26-gauge wire tails.

9 Grasp the ring in your nondominant hand, holding it on one side of the bead cap. Grasp the free 18-gauge wire end and wrap it around the ring shank four times, next to the bead cap (Figure 5).

10 Resize and reshape the ring on the mandrel.

11 Repeat Step 9 but make one wrap on the ring shank, then place the ring back on the mandrel to size it again. Repeat this process for each wrap made. Because the wire being wrapped is part of the ring shank wire, it's easy to pull the shank smaller than the desired size.

12 Trim both wire tails. If the edges are sharp, file them smooth, then use nylon-jaw pliers to gently squeeze the wire ends tight (Figure 6).

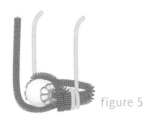

figure 5

figure 6

VARIATION
Any color or type of focal bead works great for this ring design.

○ BEGINNER

● INTERMEDIATE

○ ADVANCED

venetian
WINDOWS BRACELET

Make this sophisticated bracelet that features window-like bead frames. The coiled wire paired with the framed Venetian glass is reminiscent of an Italian promenade, complete with shop windows!

DESIGN INSPIRATION

I originally made this bracelet with fine silver beads, and while wearing the bracelet, it struck me that the beads look like windows. My original bracelet does not have bead frames, but I just had to implement them into the design.

PROJECT NOTES

Since the 22-gauge wire needs to fit through the bead hole twice, use large-holed beads. I used Venetian glass, and although molds are used during this type of bead's fabrication, they aren't always perfectly square, and the holes may vary in size. Because of this, you may want to buy a few extra.

The materials and instructions for this bracelet yield an 8" (20.3 cm) bracelet. Because of the displacement created by the square beads, this bracelet is equivalent to a fitted bracelet measuring 7½" (19.1 cm). The length of the bracelet can be changed by making the curve of the coils larger or smaller, by using smaller or larger beads, using a smaller or larger hook, or by changing the length of the coils in between each bead.

FINISHED SIZE

8" (20.3 cm)

MATERIALS

38" (96.5 cm) of 22-gauge half-hard wire

15' to 16' (4.6 m to 4.9 m) of 26-gauge dead-soft wire

10 square 10mm Venetian glass beads

10 square 14mm bead frames

1" (2.5 cm) Woven Hook clasp (page 78)

TOOLS

Flush cutters

Round-nose pliers

Chain-nose pliers

Ruler

Nylon-jaw wire-straightening pliers

TECHNIQUES USED

Coiling (page 20)

1. Cut 3" (7.6 cm) of 22-gauge wire to be used as a coiling mandrel.

2. Cut a segment of 26-gauge wire, whatever length you are comfortable working with, and make a coil on the mandrel measuring ¾" (1.9 cm). Remove the coil from the mandrel. Trim one wire tail at the coil and leave the second tail 2" (5.1 cm) long (Figure 1). Repeat to form a total of eighteen ¾" (1.9 cm) coils.

3. Form one 1½" (3.8 cm) coil with 2" (5.1 cm) tails on both ends.

4. Cut 35" (88.9 cm) of 22-gauge half-hard wire.

5. Slide the 1½" (3.8 cm) coil to the center of the 22-gauge wire.

6. Slide a frame and bead onto one end of the 22-gauge wire.

7. Feed the second end of the 22-gauge wire through opposite side of the frame and bead so the wire crisscrosses.

8. Pull both 22-gauge wire ends until the frame is against the coil, keeping the coil centered so there are equal lengths of wire on each side of the frame and bead (Figure 2).

9. Slide a ¾" (1.9 cm) piece of coil onto each 22-gauge wire end with the tail end last, pushing both coils against the frame (Figure 3).

10. Repeat Steps 6–9 until all frames, beads, and coils have been added (Figure 4).

11. Shape the coils by holding the beads on each side of one set of coils and rocking the coils back and forth while pushing them in. This will curve the coils and make wrapping in Steps 12 and 13 easier.

12. Starting with the first coil strung onto the 22-gauge wire in Step 5, wrap the tail three times around the junction of the two coils next to the frame. Don't pull hard on your wrap, or the coils will separate. Repeat on the second side (Figure 5).

13. After the third wrap, bring the wire between the coils and trim the tail. If necessary, use chain-nose pliers or your fingernail to tuck the wire end between the coils to hide it.

14. Repeat Steps 12 and 13 for all but the last two tails.

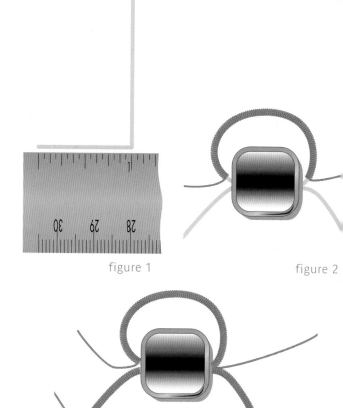

figure 1

figure 2

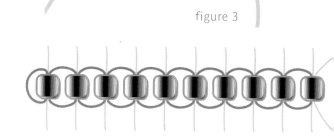

figure 3

figure 4

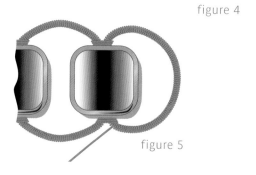

figure 5

1 5 Use your fingers to shape the two 22-gauge wire ends into a circle that matches the circle at the other end of the bracelet.

1 6 Cut 2' (61 cm) of 26-gauge wire. Hold the 22-gauge wires so that one wire is on top of the other. Leaving a 1' (30.5 cm) tail, begin coiling the center of the loop (Figure 6).

1 7 Bend the bracelet in half, holding the ending loop over the beginning loop to check that the two loops are the same size.

1 8 Adjust the loop size by using chain-nose pliers to first pull one end of the 22-gauge tail, then the other end. Check the size again. If necessary, pull the wire ends to continue adjusting the loop size. This does not need to be the exact size, but as close as possible.

1 9 Continue coiling the first half of the two 22-gauge wires, working as close to the bead frame as possible. Check the size of the loop again and, if necessary, pull a 22-gauge wire end to adjust the size smaller. Don't trim the tails yet.

2 0 Use the 1' (30.5 cm) tail to coil the second half of the two 22-gauge wires as close to the bead frame as possible (Figure 7).

2 1 Pull tightly on the 22-gauge wire ends to make sure the coiling is tight. Trim one 22-gauge tail, then continue coiling as close to the bead frame as possible. Trim the 26-gauge tail.

2 2 Repeat Step 21 for the second half of the loop.

2 3 Wrap the remaining 2" (5.1 cm) tail around the junction of the two coils next to the frame three times, repeating Steps 12 and 13. Don't pull hard on the wrap, or the coils will separate. Repeat on the second side.

2 4 Attach the Woven Hook to the end of the bracelet.

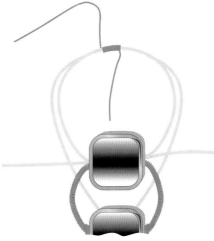

figure 6

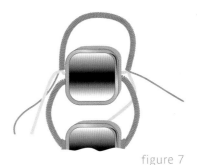

figure 7

○ BEGINNER

● INTERMEDIATE

○ ADVANCED

woven
HOOK

This beautiful woven-wire hook is the perfect finishing touch to any piece of jewelry, adding elegance to woven-wire pieces.

DESIGN INSPIRATION

I wanted to design a hook that could be used on the woven bracelets that would not catch on the weave when hooking the bracelet. I first tried a hook with spiraled ends, but that required a large space to fit through, and the weave had to stop quite short on the bracelet—too short for my liking—so I scratched that idea. This design is smooth and not obtrusive and can also function as a necklace bail.

PROJECT NOTES

Round-nose pliers having tapered barrels create an uneven loop when rolling two pieces of wire at the same time. In this project, the end of the hook is rolled in Step 11, creating an uneven roll, but there's an easy fix to this by rolling both sides of the hook. If you own round-nose pliers with barrels that are not tapered, they are ideal for this project.

FINISHED SIZE

30 mm

MATERIALS

4" (10.2 cm) of 16-gauge dead-soft wire

4' (1.2 m) of 26-gauge dead-soft wire

TOOLS

Flush cutters

Chain-nose pliers

Round-nose pliers

6 mm mandrel

Nylon-jaw wire-straightening pliers

Ruler

Permanent marking pen

TECHNIQUES USED

Wire Weaving (page 16)

Coiling (page 20)

1. Straighten the 16-gauge wire. Use the pen to mark the center of the wire.

2. Use the 6 mm mandrel to bend the wire into a U shape at the mark.

figure 1

3. Gently squeeze the wires together to check that the wire ends are the same lengths. If they aren't equal, trim the longer wire so it's the same length as the shorter wire. Even a 1 mm difference can make the hook sit crooked on your jewelry, so trim them evenly.

4. Use the tips of round-nose pliers to form a loop at each wire end. Be sure to make these loops large enough to fit over the frame of the jewelry to which it's being attached.

figure 2

5. Angle the small loops out by using chain-nose pliers to grasp each loop and make a slight bend outward (Figure 1). **NOTE:** The loops can be bent so they are parallel to each other, but you'll need to attach the hook with a jump ring because once the hook is coiled and woven, you won't be able to open the loops.

figure 3

6. Use chain-nose pliers to grasp the wire next to the loops. Make a small bend to angle the hook (Figure 2).

7. Use the 26-gauge wire to coil the two ends of the hook together until there's enough space to weave (Figure 3).

figure 4

8. Work Weave Pattern 1 (page 16) to weave the hook up to the curve of the U (Figure 4).

9. Coil the remainder of the U (Figure 5).

10. Carefully trim the weaving wire tail on the inside of the frame wire. If necessary, use chain-nose pliers to carefully squeeze the end of the weaving wire against the frame wire. Tighten the coil near the beginning weaving wire tail, then trim it.

figure 5

1 1 To shape the hook, gently grasp the U-shaped end with the wide end of round-nose pliers. Roll the pliers so the hook is on the same side as the small loops made in Step 4. Because round-nose barrels are tapered, your hook will be crooked. Place the pliers on the other side of the U and slightly roll to straighten the hook. If your coils/weave become separated, push them back together with your fingernail (Figure 6).

figure 6

1 2 Attaching the hook seems simple enough, but because the hook has two loops to attach, it can be a little tricky. Open both loops outward. Attach one loop to the jewelry, then close it. It's easiest to attach it in a corner or curve of the jewelry.

figure 7

1 3 Slide the hook along the jewelry until the second loop can be angled over a corner or curve, then attach the second loop (Figure 7).

1 4 Slide the hook to the center of the jewelry and close the second loop.

MAKING A LARGER HOOK

With a couple adjustments, a larger, wider hook can easily be made. Shown here is a 1½" (3 cm) hook. To make it, I cut 4½" (11.4 cm) of 16-gauge instead of 4" (10.2 cm). I used the barrel of my permanent marker (the diameter is 1 cm) to make the U. Then, to make the hook wider at the base, I didn't bend the loops out (Step 8) but rather, measured and marked the wire at ⅜" (9 mm), measuring from the outside of the loops. Then I angled the frame wire out at the two marks and wove this part of the hook. You can see this hook on Autumn Leaf Bracelet, page 110.

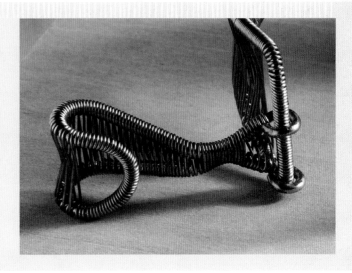

○ BEGINNER

● INTERMEDIATE

○ ADVANCED

abby's
EARRINGS

Futuristic or groovy? Create these earrings in different sizes with small and large mandrels—go small for futuristic, large for groovy—just have fun mixing up the size and wire colors.

DESIGN INSPIRATION

My dear friend Abby Hook designed a pendant called Circles and Spirals. The center frame wire of the pendant is slightly raised, which inspired me to incorporate that into one of my designs. After many trials and errors, my idea evolved into this pair of earrings, rightfully named after Abby!

PROJECT NOTES

When you need two identical frame wires for a project, it's always best to make them at the same time because you're more likely to repeat exactly what you did, such as looping your wire on the exact same spot on your round-nose pliers.

FINISHED SIZE

2" (5.1 cm)

MATERIALS

20" (50.8 cm) of 16-gauge dead-soft wire

22–24' (6.7 to 7.3 m) of 26-gauge dead-soft wire

2 ear wires

Low-stick tape

TOOLS

Round-nose pliers

Flat-nose pliers

Flush cutters

Nylon-jaw wire-straightening pliers

Bracelet mandrel

½" (1.3 cm) diameter mandrel (the barrel of a permanent marking pen works well)

Ring mandrel

Permanent marking pen

Ruler

TECHNIQUES USED

Wire Weaving (page 16)

1. Straighten and cut 10" (25.4 cm) of 16-gauge dead-soft wire. This is the frame wire.

2. Use the pen to mark the wire at 2" (5.1 cm), 5" (12.7 cm) and 8" (20.3 cm). Use flat-nose pliers to form a slight bend on the two outer marks.

3. Use the largest end of a bracelet mandrel to curve the frame wire between the bends (Figure 1).

4. Use flat-nose pliers to make a bend on the 5" (12.7 cm) mark, bringing the frame wire ends closer to each other.

5. Bend the frame wire ends out as necessary to make them parallel and touching (Figure 2). Set aside.

6. Repeat Steps 1–5 for the second earring frame wire.

7. Use some scrap 26-gauge wire to temporarily wrap the wire ends together (Figure 3).

8. Cut 6' (1.8 m) of 26-gauge wire. Coil the center of the frame wire at the 5" (12.7 cm) mark/bend, twenty to twenty-four times, centering the coil over the bend.

9. Following Weave Pattern 1 (page 16), weave back and forth four times. Trim the beginning weaving wire tail (Figure 4).

10. Tape the frame wire to the ½" (1.3 cm) mandrel. Use your fingers to shape the wire around the mandrel, pushing the frame wires down against it. Roll the mandrel on a hard flat surface to further shape the wire (Figure 5).

11. Remove the tape from the woven frame wire end. Tape the frame wire in one or two more spots for more stability.

12. Follow Weave Pattern 1, but instead of bringing the weaving wire underneath and over a frame wire twice, do it three times. Follow the weaving pattern to the center of the frame. End the weave by coiling twice around the frame. Don't trim the weaving wire tail. **NOTE:** If you need to add more weaving wire, coil the ending wire twice around a frame wire. Add new wire to it and weave across and back on the frame wires. Tighten both weaving wire tails, then remove the frame from the ½" (1.3 cm) mandrel. Trim both weaving wire tails. Retape the frame to the ½" (1.3 cm) mandrel and continue weaving.

13. Once you reach the frame's center, it's necessary to start a new weave from the opposite end, weaving to the center. You'll want to do this because the frame wires are angled,

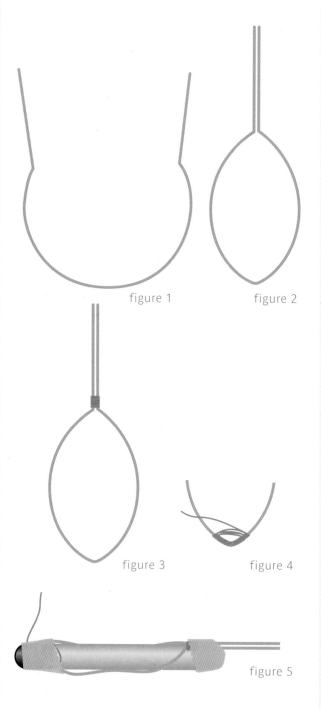

figure 1

figure 2

figure 3

figure 4

figure 5

and when weaving from a larger to smaller width, the weaving wire slips on the frame wire, making it challenging to maintain a tight, even weave.

Remove the weaving from the ½" (1.3 cm) mandrel. Remove the temporary coil from the frame wire ends. Cut 6' (1.8 m) of 26-gauge wire. Coil the frame wire ends and weave eight to ten times. Following Weave Pattern 1, weave back and forth four times (Figure 6).

figure 6

14 Tape the woven end of the earring to the mandrel, then repeat Step 12, weaving to the center of the earring. Stop weaving at the mirror point from the first side, coiling twice around the frame wire.

15 Tighten both weaving wire tails, then remove the earring from the ½" (1.3 cm) mandrel. Cut both tails.

16 Shape the earring by centering it against the smallest end of a bracelet mandrel and carefully pushing down on both ends.

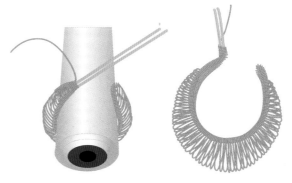

17 Center the earring against the largest end of a ring mandrel and push the ends around the mandrel (Figure 7).

figure 7   figure 8

18 Use flat-nose pliers to bend the wire ends at a 90° angle to form the top of the earring (Figure 8).

19 Slide the earring onto the ring mandrel and continue to shape it until it makes a near complete loop.

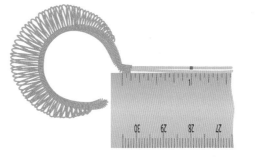

20 Tighten the coil from Step 13, then cut the 26-gauge wire tail.

21 Use the pen to mark one of the 16-gauge wire tails at 1½" (3.8 cm), measuring from the base of the coil (Figure 9). Flush cut the wire on this mark.

figure 9

22 Use the tips of round-nose pliers to form a loop of the wire just cut. Continue looping around one-quarter of a turn to form an open spiral (Figure 10).

23 Use nylon-jaw wire-straightening pliers or flat-nose pliers to move the loop to the center front of the earring.

24 Make a 90° bend at the top of the coil perpendicular to the earring on the second 16-gauge wire (Figure 11).

25 Measure and flush cut the wire as needed. Form a simple loop.

figure 10   figure 11

26 Attach an ear wire to the simple loop.

27 Repeat Steps 7–26 to form the second earring.

○ BEGINNER

● INTERMEDIATE

○ ADVANCED

ribbon
CUFF

Fabricate this undulating bracelet using frame wires woven together. The bold beads not only make this ribbon-like cuff extra pretty, but add structural elements as well.

DESIGN INSPIRATION

I wanted to design a bracelet that would stand up from the wrist. My daughter was wrapping a birthday gift for a friend, and when she curled the ribbon, this idea struck me. After multiple attempts and lots of measuring, shaping, and tossing copper wire, I finally created this "ribbon" with wire.

PROJECT NOTES

You can use round-nose pliers as a mandrel for this project, but the mandrel must have a larger diameter than the beads. That means a 5 or 6 mm mandrel will work for 4mm or 6mm beads; a 7 or 8 mm mandrel will work for 6mm or 8mm beads, etc. I used a 10 mm mandrel (the handle of a crochet hook) with 9mm blue agate beads.

FINISHED SIZE

6" (15.2 cm), adjustable

MATERIALS

16' to 18' (4.9 m to 5.5 m) of 26-gauge dead-soft wire

28" (71.1 cm) of 16-gauge dead-soft wire

3 round beads (size is determined by the round-nose pliers or mandrel being used)

Low-stick tape

TOOLS

Flush cutters

Round-nose pliers

Round mandrel

Chain-nose pliers

Nylon-jaw wire-straightening pliers

Ruler

Permanent marking pen

Bracelet mandrel or nylon-jaw bracelet-forming pliers

TECHNIQUES USED

Wire Weaving (page 16)

1   Straighten and cut two 14" (35.6cm) pieces of 16-gauge wire. Mark the center of each wire.

2   Use the mandrel to bend one of the wires into a U shape on the mark.

3   Hold the mandrel against the side of the U's curve, then slightly roll and pull the wire around the mandrel to form another U.

4   Repeat Step 3 two more times, taking care to keep the bends as uniform as possible.

5   Place round-nose pliers into the last loop made and form a bend 90° to the final curve.

6   Form curves on the other half of the wire by holding the mandrel against the other side of the center U shape and repeating Step 3 three times. Repeat Step 5 (Figure 1). This is one of the frame wires. Set aside.

7   Use the second piece of 16-gauge wire to repeat Steps 2–6.

8   Use a 6" (15.2 cm) piece of scrap 26-gauge wire to temporarily coil a bead at the base of the first curve on one of the frame wires, leaving a 3" (7.6 cm) tail. Weave back and forth two to three times, attaching the second frame wire. Use the tail wire to weave back and forth two to three times so there is a temporary weave on both sides of the bead.

Trim the 26-gauge wire tails. **NOTE:** You place the bead to help keep the wires appropriately spaced while weaving the cuff.

9   Squeeze each set of frame wire ends together so they touch. Tape the ends in place.

10 Repeat Step 8 to temporarily wrap a second bead between the frame wires (Figure 2). **NOTE:** The 2 beads will not keep your frame wires from angling in as you weave, but are a guide for spacing. It's important while weaving to check the alignment of your frame wires frequently, ensuring they aren't angling inward, but remaining vertical. If your frame wires angle in toward each other, realign them by placing a chain-nose pliers between the frame wires and gently pushing the pliers open.

11 Tape the frame wires next to the first bead added. Cut 4' to 5' (1.2 m to 1.5 m) of 26-gauge wire and coil twice around one of the frame wires between the 2 beads. Begin Weave Pattern 1 (page 16) (Figure 3).

12 Continue to weave to just before the center of the first curve's bottom. Slide the second temporary bead along the frames wires until it reaches the bottom of the next curve.

13 String a bead onto the weaving wire. Continue with Weave Pattern 1, weaving under the bead (Figure 4). Add more weaving wire as needed.

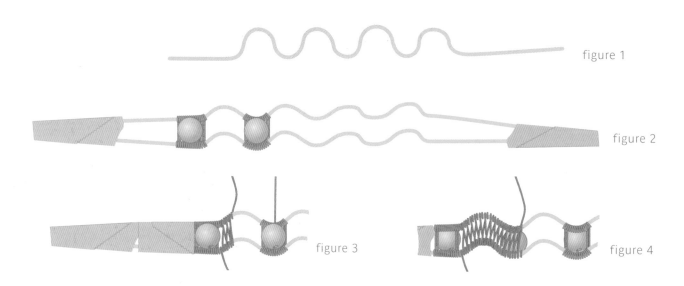

figure 1

figure 2

figure 3

figure 4

14 Repeat Steps 12 and 13 twice. Leave the second temporary bead in place on the wire frame and weave to the bottom of the last curve. Remove the first temporary bead (Figure 5).

15 Remove the second temporary bead and all tape. **NOTE:** Don't cut the wire tails yet. With the weaving wire tails still attached, it's much easier to see where the weave ends in order to blend the new weave. It's also helpful for tightening the weave if necessary.

16 Determine how much wire will be required to make the spiral ends on the frame wires (see Autumn Leaf Bracelet, page 110). If desired, forge and file/sand the spiral arches. If necessary, gently squeeze the frame wires together, so the two spirals are touching each other.

17 Measure and mark the frame wire on each side of the curved section according to your desired final cuff length. Flush cut the wires. For the 6" (15.2 cm) cuff shown, I needed 1" (2.5 cm) for each spiral end, so that's 6" (2.5 cm), plus 1" (2.5 cm), plus 1" (2.5 cm), equals 8" (20.3 cm) of frame wire. Next, I subtracted the 3" (7.6 cm) ribbon section, which equals 5" (12.7 cm). I divided 5" (12.7 cm) in half, equaling 2½" (6.4 cm): the length of wire I need on each side of the ribbon section.

18 Follow Steps 6–11 of Autumn Leaf Bracelet (page 110) to form the spiral ends (Figure 6).

19 Cut 4' to 5' (1.2 m to 1.5 m) of 26-gauge wire. Leaving a 12" (30.5 cm) tail, coil six to eight times around both frame wires where they touch. Coil until there's room to weave, then begin Weave Pattern 1 (Figure 7).

20 Weave up to the base of the curved section. As the weaving space becomes small, it becomes difficult to weave. Create more space by pulling the weave back with your fingers.

21 Blending the weaves is the same technique used to add more wire (see Adding Weaving Wire, Weave Patterns 1, 2, 3, and 4, page 19). Use the weaving wire tail to coil just once around the frame wire. Pull the wire tail tightly (you won't be able to complete Steps 3 and 4 of Adding Weaving Wire), then trim. End the weave from Steps 19 and 20 next to this cut. Coil the wire just once around the frame wire, pulling tightly, then trim.

22 Use the 12" (30.5 cm) wire tail to coil around the spiral ends six to eight times until there is room to weave (Figure 8).

23 Work Weave Pattern 1 to the curves of the spiral ends. Trim the wire tail (Figure 9).

24 Repeat Steps 19–23 for the second half of the cuff frame.

25 Form the cuff using a bracelet mandrel or nylon-jaw bracelet-forming pliers.

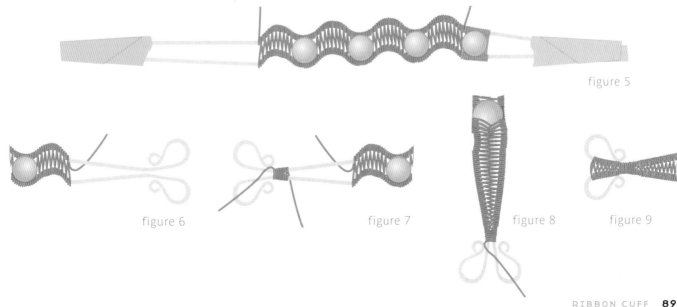

figure 5

figure 6

figure 7

figure 8

figure 9

BEGINNER

● INTERMEDIATE

ADVANCED

grecian urn
PENDANT

A podlike shape hangs gracefully from a handmade chain, evoking the small amphora of a Greek goddess. The pendant is deceivingly simple to make by connecting three wire frames with an easy coiling pattern.

DESIGN INSPIRATION

I was having a dilemma with what to name this pendant. Its original name was Pod Pendant; how boring! But when I got to Step 16 and was forming the open loops, it struck me: Grecian Urn. My sister Misti and I evidently have a great fondness for Greek and Roman art, as she named the Caesar's Scrolls Bracelet.

PROJECT NOTES

Parallel pliers have barrels that close parallel to each other, so they are a great tool for removing any small lumps in wire by gently squeezing it. I also like to use them when I need to grasp two or more wire frames at the same time, again because of the parallel closure as opposed to a bill-like closure from flat- and chain-nose pliers.

FINISHED SIZE

6½" (16.5 cm)

MATERIALS

15" (38.1 cm) of 18-gauge dead-soft wire

7' to 8' (2.1 m to 2.4 m) of 26-gauge dead-soft wire

18¾" (47.6 cm) commercial or handmade chain (page 14)

1 handmade 34mm Spiral Hook (page 15) or commercial toggle clasp

4 round 6mm 16-gauge jump rings (if toggle clasp is used)

TOOLS

Flush cutters

Round-nose pliers

Chain-nose pliers

Flat-nose pliers

Parallel pliers

Nylon-jaw wire-straightening pliers

Ring mandrel

Ruler

Permanent marking pen

TECHNIQUES USED

Wire Weaving (page 16)

Coiling (page 20)

1. Straighten and flush cut three 5" (12.7 cm) pieces of 18-gauge wire. These are the frame wires. Mark each wire at 1" (2.5 cm), 2⅜" (6 cm), 2⅝" (6.7 cm), and 4" (10.2 cm).

2. Cut 1' (30.5 cm) of 26-gauge wire. This is the weaving wire. Starting at the 2⅜" (6 cm) pen mark, coil around a frame wire once, coil the second frame wire once, then coil the third frame wire once.

3. Bring the weaving wire behind all three frame wires and coil the first frame wire one time.

4. Coil the second and third frame wires once each, then repeat Step 3, coiling up to the second pen mark (Figure 1). This is the base of the pendant. **NOTE:** In the following steps as you shape the pendant, the coil wire ends may loosen. For this reason, don't cut the tails yet. Once the shaping is complete, the coil ends can be tightened, then cut.

5. Hold an outer frame wire of the coiled section against size 1 on the ring mandrel so the pen marks are visible. Shape the wire around the mandrel until its ends touch (Figure 2).

6. Move the coiled section up so the middle frame wire is on size 1. Shape the middle wire around the mandrel until its ends touch.

7. Repeat Step 6 for the third frame wire (Figure 3).

8. Use flat-nose pliers to bend a 90° angle next to the coil end of an outside frame wire.

9. Make a second 90° bend next to the second coil end on the same wire.

10. Repeat Steps 8–9 on the second outer frame wire. Turn the frame wires so the wire ends come together (Figure 4).

11. Align the frame wires by holding onto the coiled section with parallel pliers and gently bending the wires with your fingers to center the wires (Figure 5).

12. Starting with the center frame wire, form slight bends at the 1" (2.5 cm) and 4" (10.2 cm) marks made in Step 1 so that the top of the frame wires are parallel to each other. Repeat for the two outer frame wires (Figure 6).

13. Straighten the coiled base by gently squeezing it with parallel pliers. This will also align the wire ends. If necessary, flush cut the wire ends so they are all the same length.

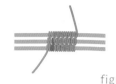

figure 1

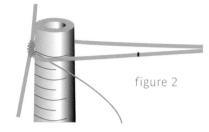

figure 2

figure 3

figure 4

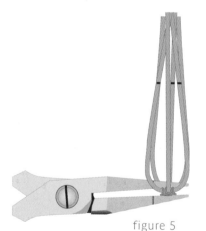

figure 5

14 Use the tips of round-nose pliers to form a loop on each wire end, continuing to loop around one-quarter turn to create an open spiral, so the loops are facing outward from the center of the pod. The loops need to be parallel to each other. If necessary, bend the frame wires again so they are parallel to each other after making the loops (Figure 7).

15 Cut 5' (1.5 m) of 26-gauge wire. Coil the looped frame wires together ten to fourteen times until there's enough space between the frame wires to weave (Figure 8—red wire). At this point, the coiled base wire tails from Steps 2–4 can be trimmed. If necessary, pull each wire tail to ensure the coil is tight before trimming.

16 Coil one time around a frame wire. Don't bring the wire underneath the next frame wire as normally done in Weave Pattern 1 but rather bring the wire over the top of the next frame wire, then coil around the next frame wire once, then coil around the next frame wire once (Figure 8—blue wire).

17 Continue coiling around each frame wire one time, continuously working your way around the pendant (Figure 8—brown wire). As you weave around the frame, be sure to check the alignment of the wires, as pulling on the weaving wire can misalign the frame wires. If they became misaligned, use chain-nose pliers to gently bend them back into alignment.

18 To add additional weaving wire, coil once around a frame wire. Don't cut the wire tail. With the new piece of weaving wire, coil once around the same frame wire, then coil around the next two or three frame wires. Pull the ending weaving wire tail tightly, then cut it on the inside of the frame wire. It's a little tricky, but if your cutters are pointed, it's possible. Likewise, pull the new weaving wire tightly, cutting the tail on the inside of the frame wires.

19 As you near the coil base and the spacing between the frame wires becomes small, make a bend in the end of the weaving wire for ease of threading the wire around a frame wire.

20 Continue coiling around each frame wire to the coil base (Figure 9), then cut the weaving wire tail.

21 Use your fingers to separate and open the top loops of the two outside frame wires as desired (Figure 10). Tighten and trim the beginning wire tail.

22 Attach one chain length to each of the two middle frame wire open loops. Connect the clasp to the chain ends.

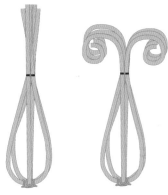

figure 6   figure 7

figure 8

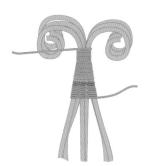

figure 9

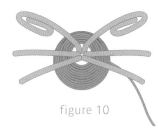

figure 10

○ BEGINNER

○ INTERMEDIATE

● ADVANCED

vogue
RING

Woven wires and beads swirl together to form this stately ring. Change up the wire type and beads, and you've created something truly your own.

DESIGN INSPIRATION

This is one of the first woven rings that I ever made. I was experimenting to see what I could come up with, not having any solid idea in mind. I was delightfully surprised when I ended up with this ring as my final design on my first try! Sometimes designs significantly evolve from the starting point of what we have sketched or thought the outcome would be. Maybe this turned out well the first time because I just dove right in.

PROJECT NOTES

I would advise against using glass or crystal beads for this project. They are really too delicate to withstand the construction of the ring. Another consideration for bead selection is what will fit on the 16-gauge wire. Thai beads and African trade beads are good choices since they typically have large holes.

Please note that the measurements for this ring are for size 6½ or 7. I have noted in the steps where to change lengths if you want to make a different size, but when you make it the first time, follow the steps as directed so you get a feel for the construction of the ring.

FINISHED SIZE

28 x15 mm (ring top)

MATERIALS

28" (71.1 cm) of 16-gauge dead-soft wire

10½' (3.2 m) of 26-gauge dead-soft wire

8 large-holed 3mm beads

TOOLS

Flush cutters

Chain-nose pliers

Nylon-jaw wire-straightening pliers

Ring mandrel

File

Ruler

Permanent marking pen

TECHNIQUES USED

Wire Weaving (page 16)

Coiling (page 20)

1. Cut three 8" (20.3 cm) pieces of 16-gauge wire. These are Frame Wires 1, 2, and 3.

2. Make marks on Frame Wire 1 at 3½" (8.9 cm) and 4½" (11.4 cm). These marks are a guide for the bead placement on the ring shank.

3. Cut 4' (1.2 m) of 26-gauge wire.

4. Coil the 26-gauge wire two to three times around Frame Wire 1 at one of the marks made in Step 2 (Figure 1—red wire).

5. Slide a bead onto Frame Wire 2. **NOTE:** The bead is placed to keep the wires appropriately spaced apart. Use Weave Pattern 4 (see page 18) to connect Frame Wire 2 to Frame Wire 1, just to the left of the bead.

6. Hold Frame Wire 3 parallel to Frame Wire 2. Coil Frame Wire 3 the width of the bead (Figure 1—blue wire).

7. Slide a bead onto Frame Wire 2 and weave the wire to the left of the bead, thereby securing the previous bead added. This is a bit awkward, but it really does keep the wire spaced correctly. **NOTE:** It helps to slide the bead up the frame wire, loosely wrap the weaving wire around, let the bead slide back down to the weaving wire, then tighten up the weaving wire.

8. Weave around Frame Wire 1, then coil Frame Wire 1 the remaining width of the bead added in Step 7 (Figure 1—brown wire).

9. Repeat Step 7.

10. Repeat Steps 6–9 to add a total of 6 beads, ending with Step 8.

11. Slide a bead onto Frame Wire 2, again to keep the wires appropriately spaced. Continue working Weave Pattern 4 to the left of the bead just added, connecting Frame Wires 2 and 3, then 2 and 1 one time each (Figure 2).

12. There should be 3½" (8.9 cm) of bare frame wire on the left. Adjust the position of the bead/weave section as necessary, placing it at this mark if things shifted while weaving.

13. Leave the bead on Frame Wire 2 for spacing and follow Weave Pattern 1, connecting Frame Wires 1 and 2 for ⅜" (9 mm). (To make a larger or smaller ring, increase or decrease this measurement. All of the following measurements for coiling and weaving lengths would need to be

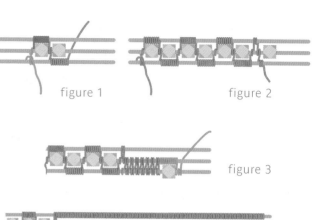

figure 1

figure 2

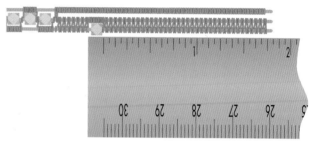

figure 3

figure 4

figure 5

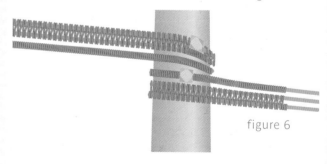

figure 6

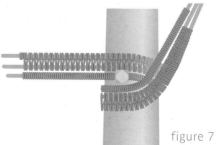

figure 7

changed to reflect this change.) Periodically adjust the bead/weave section as necessary.

14 Remove the end bead from Frame Wire 2 and place it on Frame Wire 1. Coil Frame Wire 2 the length of the bead, then coil Frame Wire 1 one time (Figure 3—red wire).

15 Place a bead on Frame Wire 2, again to keep the wires appropriately spaced. Resume Weave Pattern 1, connecting Frame Wires 1 and 2 an additional 1¼" (3.2 cm). Remove the bead and trim the weaving wire tails.

16 Cut 3" (7.6 cm) of 16-gauge wire to use as a mandrel. Cut 2½' (76.2 cm) of 26-gauge wire. Coil 1¾" (4.5 cm), remove from mandrel and trim wire tails, then slide the coil onto Frame Wire 3 (Figure 4).

17 Cut 4' (1.2 m) of 26-gauge wire.

18 Turn the frame upside down so that Frame Wire 1 is now Frame Wire 3 and vice versa. Slide a bead on Frame Wire 2 for spacing. Following Weave Pattern 1, connect Frame Wires 1 and 2 for 1¾" (4.5 cm). Remove the bead and trim both weaving wire tails.

19 Use the remaining piece of 26-gauge wire from Step 18 to coil ¾" (1.9 cm) on the 16-gauge wire mandrel. Trim the weaving wire tails.

20 Slide a bead on Frame Wire 3, then make a coil on the 16-gauge wire mandrel the same length of the weave made in Step 18 for about 1" (2.5 cm). Remove the coil from the mandrel and trim wire tails, then slide the coil onto Frame Wire 3 (Figure 5).

21 If desired, antique the weaving.

22 Center the 6 beads on size 6½ or 7 of the ring mandrel. Wrap each side of the ring around the mandrel, being sure to wrap the coiled/beaded sections of each side of the frame so they end up being the middle wires on the ring (Figure 6).

23 Use your fingers to guide the non-bead coiled wire around the side of the center bead on the beaded coiled wire.

24 Guide the woven section so it sits next to the coiled wire placed in the previous step (Figure 7).

25 Remove the ring from the mandrel, turn it over, and slide it back onto the mandrel. Guide the coiled and woven frame wires up the other side of the center bead.

26 Remove the ring from the mandrel. Pull the coiled wire through the ring shank, then pull the woven wire through the shank.

27 Repeat Step 26 for the second set of frame wires (Figure 8). Size your ring. **NOTE:** As you shape the ring, it's easy to pull the shank smaller than the desired size, so be sure to size your ring after the each of the following steps. Also, it's likely the coiling and weaving will move on the frame wire, so be sure to push it back, eliminating spaces that might develop in the coil or weave.

Work one side of the frame wires, then the second side. Pull the set of wires through the ring shank one wire at a time. Size the ring, then repeat on the second side of frame wires, again pulling one wire through at a time.

28 Wrap the frame wires at one side of the ring around the ring shank again, working with one wire at a time. When all three frame wires are pulled up on the first side, repeat on the second side (Figure 9).

29 Pull the set of wires wire through the ring shank one at a time, then pull the second set of wires through the ring shank (Figure 10).

30 Size the ring and trim all frame wire tails. If the edges are sharp, file them smooth. Squeeze the ends down with nylon-jaw pliers.

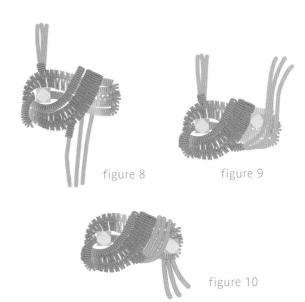

figure 8

figure 9

figure 10

venetian
HILL TRIBE BRACELET

This design is perfect for featuring a special focal bead. The way the coils frame the bead and the cuff flares out from the sides evokes an eye-catching treat!

DESIGN INSPIRATION

This bracelet is a spinoff of my Hill Tribe Bracelet, which was the beginning of my adventure into weaving wire jewelry. I designed this because I wanted a bracelet that could be worn as a cuff or as a bracelet with a hook, which led to the design of my Woven Hook (page 78). The tapered design structure next to the bead, as opposed to the squared off design of the Hill Tribe, allows this to function as a cuff while still being able to add a hook for a bracelet, if desired. I love how one idea leads to another!

PROJECT NOTES

Ovals, coins, and round-shaped beads are all good choices for the focal bead, with oval being the best shape to start with. Pick a bead that measures, hole to hole, 2 cm to 3 cm long. The width of the bead should be 1.5 cm to 3 cm at its widest point. The Venetian bead used for this tutorial is 17 x 28 mm.

FINISHED SIZE

6½" (16.5 cm)

MATERIALS

28" (71 cm) of 16-gauge dead-soft wire

23' to 25' (7 to 7.6 m) of 26-gauge dead-soft wire

1 flat oval 17 x 28mm focal bead (see Project Notes at left)

TOOLS

Chain-nose pliers

Flat-nose pliers

Flush cutters

Nylon-jaw wire-straightening pliers

Parallel pliers

Ruler

Permanent marking pen

Bracelet mandrel

TECHNIQUES USED

Wire Weaving (page 16)

Coiling (page 20)

1. Determine the length of each side of your cuff by subtracting the length of the focal bead and ½" (1.3 cm) (for the center wraps) from the desired finish length, then split that figure in half. For example, the bracelet shown is 6½" (16.5 cm) (length of bracelet) minus 1½" (3.8 cm) (focal bead + ½" [1.3 cm] wrapping space) equals 5" (12.7 cm), divided by 2 equals 2½" (6.4 cm). This tells me that each side of my cuff is 2½" (6.4 cm).

2. Use the pen to mark the center of the 16-gauge wire.

3. Place the focal bead next to the wire, centered over the mark. Mark the wire ¼" (6 mm) on each side of the focal bead.

4. Use flat-nose pliers to make a slight bend at one of the outside marks made in Step 3.

5. Measuring from the bend, mark the wire the length figured in Step 1. Make a 90° bend at this mark.

6. Measure ¾" (1.9 cm) from the bend made in Step 5, mark the wire, and make a 90° bend at the mark.

7. Measuring from the mark made in Step 6, mark your wire the length figured in Step 1. Bend the wire on the mark so that it crosses over the mark made in Step 4 (Figure 1).

8. Hold the frame with parallel pliers, then wrap the wire one full loop around the center wire. Don't cut the wire tail (Figure 2).

9. Slide the bead onto the wire and repeat Steps 4–8.

10. Wrap each wire tail next to, or as close to, the focal bead as possible. Wrap one tail one time around the center wire,

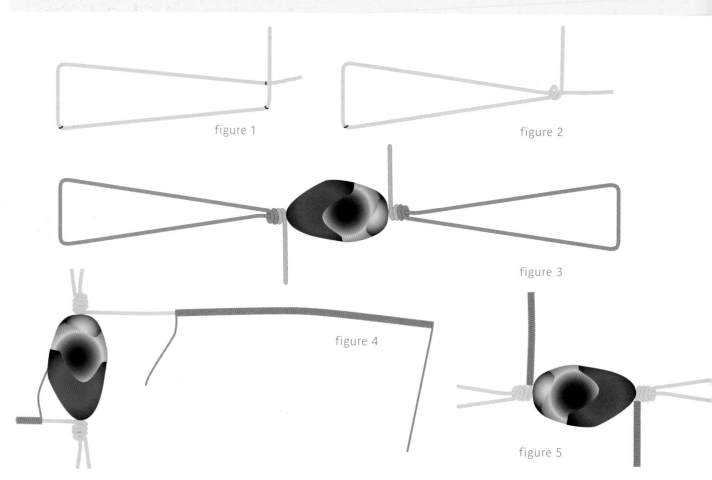

figure 1

figure 2

figure 3

figure 4

figure 5

then wrap the second tail one time around. Repeat this as often as required until the wire on both sides is against or close to the center bead (Figure 3). The most important thing is to end up with the wires on the bottom of the frame and facing in opposite directions.

1 1 Cut 3½' (1.1 m) of 26-gauge wire. Leaving a 1" (2.5 cm) tail, coil one of the 16-gauge wire tails. Leave a 2" (5.1 cm) ending tail. Repeat for the second 16-gauge wire tail (Figure 4).

1 2 Push one coil as close as possible to the wrapping done in Step 10. Wrap the beginning 1" (2.5 cm) tail around the 16-gauge wrap. This secures the coil and prevents it from sliding when wrapping the coiled 16-gauge wire around the focal bead. Trim the beginning 26-gauge wire tail but don't trim the end tail yet. Repeat this for the second coil (Figure 5).

1 3 Pull one of the 16-gauge wire tails over the top side of the focal bead, then pull the second tail under the bottom side (Figure 6).

1 4 Wrap one 16-gauge coiled tail over the wrap made in Step 10 two to four times. If necessary, uncoil the 16-gauge wire so that when you trim the tail, you cut uncoiled 16-gauge wire. (It's easier to squeeze the end down if it's not coiled.)

Wrap the 26-gauge wire tail one time around the coiled wrap, pulling the wire so it's tucked within the coiled wrap. Trim the 26- and 16-gauge wire tails. Repeat on the second side (Figure 7).

1 5 Cut 4' (1.2 m) of 26-gauge wire. Coil around the frame six to eight times until there's room to weave.

1 6 Work Weave Pattern 1 (page 16), weaving as close to the end of the frame as possible (Figure 8).

1 7 Coil around the remaining frame, then trim the weaving wire tail on the inside of the frame (Figure 9). If necessary, use chain-nose pliers to press the weaving wire end against the frame. If necessary, tighten the coil made in Step 15, then trim the working wire tail.

1 8 Repeat Steps 15–17.

1 9 Shape the cuff on a bracelet mandrel or with a nylon-jaw bracelet-forming pliers.

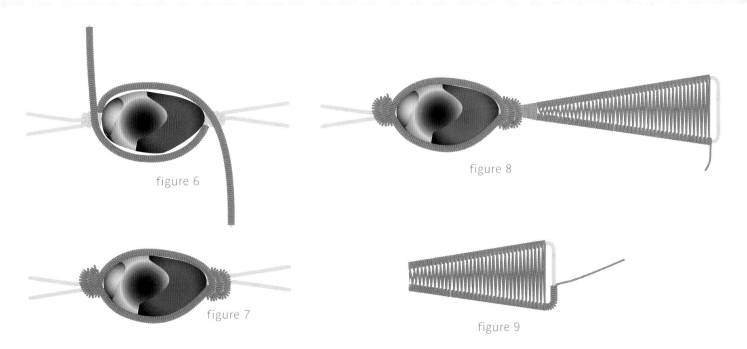

figure 6

figure 7

figure 8

figure 9

○ BEGINNER

○ INTERMEDIATE

● ADVANCED

evolution
RING

This elegant ring features two different weave patterns flanked by fluid wire lines. A central ametrine bead provides the interesting focal piece for this version, but any bead will do.

DESIGN INSPIRATION

I first named this ring Brass and Ametrine Ring but changed it to Evolution Ring because I made the ring six times, six different ways, before I was able to design what I had in mind, each time getting a bit closer, until finally, aha! I have all my prototypes lined up on my jewelry bench, in order, from inception to finish to see the progression. It's always such a great feeling when a design idea hits the mark on the first or second try, which happens from time to time, but working this ring six times just makes me appreciate it all the more!

PROJECT NOTES

The focal bead hole needs to be wide enough for the 26-gauge wire to pass through twice. With its flat sides, a rondelle-shaped bead is the best choice for this ring as the sides sit flush to the frame wire.

This ring can also be made with 18-gauge wire.

FINISHED SIZE

10 x 26mm (ring top)

MATERIALS

28" (71.1 cm) of 16-gauge dead-soft wire

5' (1.5 m) of 26-gauge dead-soft wire

1 rondelle 4mm or 6mm bead

TOOLS

Flush cutters

Chain-nose pliers

Nylon-jaw wire-straightening pliers

Ring mandrel

Ruler

Permanent marking pen

File

TECHNIQUES USED

Wire Weaving (page 16)

Coiling (page 20)

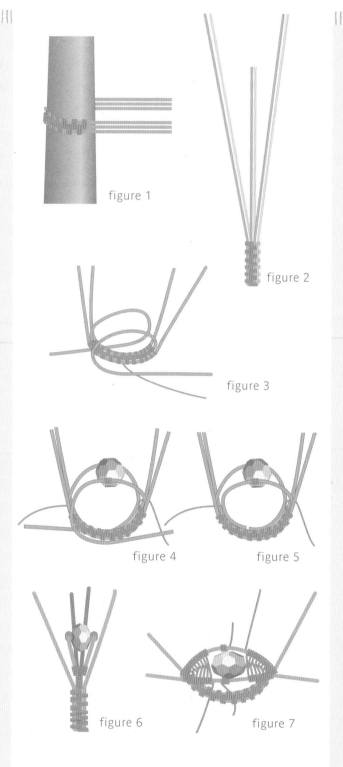

1. Cut two 10" (25.4 cm) pieces of 16-gauge wire (Frame Wires 1 and 3) and one 8" (20.3 cm) piece of 16-gauge wire (Frame Wire 2). Use the pen to mark Frame Wires 1 and 3 at 4¼" (10.8 cm) and 5¾" (14.6 cm). Mark Frame Wire 2 at 3¼" (8.3 cm) and 4¾" (12.1 cm). These are guiding marks for weaving. **NOTE:** The measurements and directions for this ring will yield a ring sized from 6 to 8. To make a smaller ring, change the wire marks to 4⅜" (11.1 cm) and 5⅝" (14.4 cm) and 3⅜" (8.6 cm) and 4⅝" (11.8 cm). Likewise, you'll weave ¼" (6 mm) less in Step 4. Keep in mind that a smaller ring is harder to make and also makes the top of the ring bulky.

2. Cut 5' (1.5 m) of 26-gauge wire.

3. Coil one time around a Frame Wire 1 on one of the marks made in Step 1, leaving a 2' (61 cm) 26-gauge beginning wire tail.

4. Work Weave Pattern 5 (page 18) for 1½" (3.8 cm), incorporating Frame Wires 2 and 3 and beginning the weave on the marks made in Step 1. Don't cut the weaving wire tails. This weave forms the back of the ring.

5. Center the weaving against the ring mandrel so it's placed one size larger than your desired ring size. Shape the frame wires into a U (Figure 1).

6. Remove the ring from the mandrel. Bend the two outer frame wires slightly out on both ends of the U shape (Figure 2).

7. Center the weaving on the ring mandrel so it's placed one size larger than your desired ring size. Pull the center wires around the mandrel, wrapping each to the outside of the outer frame wires then around to the back of the ring shank.

8. Remove the ring from the mandrel. If necessary, bend the two center frame wires out slightly to accommodate the size of the bead (Figure 3).

9. Use a small piece of 26-gauge wire to temporarily coil the bead onto the two center frame wires (Figure 4).

10. Flush cut the two center frame wires so they end at the back center of the ring shank.

11. Use your fingers to push each frame wire tail into the center of the ring shank. Don't cut the frame wire tails yet (Figure 5).

figure 1

figure 2

figure 3

figure 4   figure 5

figure 6   figure 7

12 Use one of the 26-gauge wire tails to coil one side of the two center frame wires together until there is enough space to weave. Coil the two center frame wires on the other side together. **NOTE:** It's best to work one set of wires at a time to keep the coiling and weaving equal, which will, in turn, keep the focal bead centered.

13 Work Weave Pattern 1 (page 16), weaving one side of the two center frame wires together, then the second set. Work back and forth, weaving one side, then the second side (Figure 6).

14 Continue weaving, alternating sides, until the weave is next to the bead. There should be a weaving tail on each side of the ring. Use the pen to mark both frame wires at the bead holes (Figure 7).

15 Remove the bead.

16 Use the wire tails to coil each frame wire until you reach the pen marks. String the bead onto one weaving wire, then pass the second wire through the bead in the opposite direction (Figure 8).

17 Pull each weaving wire until the bead sits snugly between the frame wires.

18 Use the remaining 26-gauge wire tails to coil each center frame wire back to the weave. Cut the weaving wire tail on the inside of the ring (Figure 9). **NOTE:** Since one wire was tucked inside each side of the ring shank, there's a high and a low side on each side of the ring. In Figure 10, the high side is on the right and the low side on the left. On the other side of the ring, the high side is on the left with the low side on the right.

19 Place the ring on the mandrel and pull the frame wire from a low side around the bead. Pull the high side frame wire around the outside frame of the ring. Remove the ring from the mandrel, turn it over, and slide it back on. Repeat this step for the second set of frame wires.

20 Pull each set of wires so they cross the front of the ring (Figure 11).

21 Make a bend with the wire that goes around the bead at the coil/weave junction from Step 12, then wrap the wire to the inside of the ring shank. Making the bend at the coil/weave junction is a guideline to keeping the ring sides symmetrical.

22 Wrap the second wire to the inside of the ring shank. If necessary, gently squeeze the frame wires with nylon-jaw pliers to flatten them against the ring (Figure 12).

23 Repeat Steps 21 and 22 with the second set of wires.

24 On the inside of the ring shank, cut the frame wire tails from Step 11, trimming them next to the second wire wrapped in Step 22. Wrap each set of frame wires around the shank two times (Figure 13).

25 Cut all frame wire tails. If the wire edges are sharp, file them smooth. If necessary, gently squeeze the wire ends with a nylon-jaw pliers. Shape and size your ring on the mandrel.

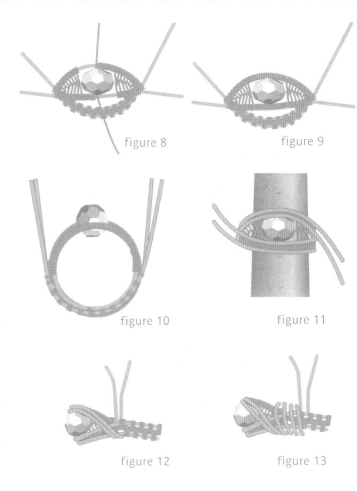

figure 8

figure 9

figure 10

figure 11

figure 12

figure 13

○ BEGINNER

○ INTERMEDIATE

● ADVANCED

illusion
CUFF

This three-dimensional cuff is visually and physically light as air! For this project, you'll set up a clever weaving mandrel to create the Slinky-like coils.

DESIGN INSPIRATION

I really wanted to design a 3-D cuff, and after many attempts, I finally came up with this design. I tried multiple times to design a cuff without a mandrel, but the designs were too boxy, and the weave actually "sunk in" in between the frame wires. Ultimately a steel mandrel was the perfect solution.

PROJECT NOTES

The size of your bead will be determined by the size of your mandrel. The width of my mandrel is 8 mm, so I used 8mm beads.

You can purchase your mandrel and file from a hardware store. The mandrel should be at least ¼" (6 mm) square. I found wood mandrels to be cut unevenly, so I don't recommend them. You'll need a metal file to slightly round one end of a steel mandrel. A jewelry file is not appropriate for this task. I used sandpaper on the shaft of the mandrel to obtain a smooth surface and remove burrs. Only 3" to 4" (7.6 to 10.2 cm) of the mandrel shaft needs to be sanded. When I bought my mandrel, I ran my fingers over several of them, feeling for burrs or divets and picked the mandrel with the least blemishes.

FINISHED SIZE

6½" (16.5 cm)

MATERIALS

14" (35.6 cm) of 16-gauge scrap brass, copper, or craft wire

34" (86.4 cm) of 16-gauge dead-soft wire

23' to 25' (7 m to 7.6 m) of 26-gauge dead-soft wire

2 round 8mm beads

TOOLS

Chain-nose pliers

Flat-nose pliers

Flush cutters

⁵/₁₆" (8 mm) diameter square steel mandrel

File

Nylon-jaw wire-straightening pliers

Bracelet mandrel

Ruler

Permanent marking pen

TECHNIQUES USED

Wire Weaving (page 16)

1   Prepare the mandrel by filing one end. It's very important to round the end of the mandrel to facilitate removing the weave from the mandrel. Sand the edges and any blemishes.

2   Use the pen to make three or four marks down the middle of the mandrel on all four sides (Figure 1).

3   Straighten the 16-gauge scrap wire. Use the pen to mark the wire at 6¾" (17.1 cm). Make a second mark the width of your mandrel from the first mark. Use flat-nose pliers to form a 90° bend on each mark. **NOTE:** This wire is woven over and not incorporated into the cuff. It's necessary in the construction of the cuff for two reasons: It adds more dimension to the overall design, and it facilitates moving the cuff off the mandrel as the weaving is completed (Figure 2).

4   Tape the bent scrap wire to the mandrel, using the pen marks as a guide to keep the wire centered. Tape the wire ends down.

5   Straighten and cut 20" (50.8 cm) of 16-gauge dead-soft wire. Use the pen to mark the wire at 9¾" (1.9 cm). Make a second mark the width of your mandrel from the first mark. Form a 90° bend on each mark. This is the cuff frame and is woven around and incorporated into the cuff.

6   Measure 2" (5.1 cm) from the bends made in Step 5 and tape the cuff frame so the tape edge is at 2" (5.1 cm). (This allows 2" (5.1 cm) of wire to work with when it's time to finish the cuff.)

7   Cut 3" (7.6 cm) of 26-gauge wire scrap wire. Coil this around the cuff frame. Remove the coil and cut it in half. Slide 1 coiled piece onto each side of the cuff frame, about 1" (2.5 cm) from the tape (Figure 3). **NOTE:** The coils keep the cuff frame elevated from the mandrel, thus facilitating weaving.

8   Tape the cuff frame onto the mandrel with the taped end from Step 6 against the end. Use the pen marks on the mandrel as a guide to center the wire. It's a good idea to tape down the ends of the cuff frame, too, just to keep them from catching on anything (Figure 4).

9   Cut 5' (1.5 m) of 26-gauge wire. Leaving a 1' (30.5 cm) wire tail, coil twice around a cuff frame wire, above the coil.

10 Pull the wire around the mandrel, then coil twice around the second side of the cuff frame. Coil over the top, not

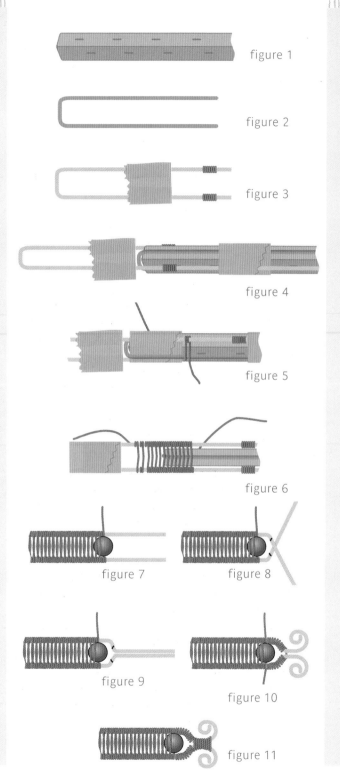

figure 1

figure 2

figure 3

figure 4

figure 5

figure 6

figure 7

figure 8

figure 9

figure 10

figure 11

under, the cuff frame wire. Check the cuff frame wire on the first side of the mandrel to ensure it's centered on the mandrel; don't trust the tape to hold the wire in alignment (Figure 5).

11 Repeat Step 10 until there is about ¾" (1.9 cm) of weave on the cuff frame.

12 Push the woven section of the cuff up and off of the mandrel. This needs to be done about every ¾" to 1" (1.9 to 2.5 cm). The more weave on the mandrel, the harder it is to push off. Remove the tape from the cuff frame only and grasp each side of the frame with your thumb and first finger and pull and/or push. Keep in mind the wires are tight and will take a little maneuvering.

13 Leave about ¼" (6 mm) of weave on the mandrel, then retape the cuff frame to the mandrel (Figure 6).

14 When more weaving wire is necessary, coil the ending wire one time around a frame wire. Coil the new weaving wire one time around the same frame wire. Coil the new weaving wire two times around the next frame wire. Pull the ending weaving wire tail to tighten the coil, then cut the wire tail as close to the underside of the frame as possible. Repeat for the new wire tail.

Coil the new weaving wire around the next frame, then push the weave together tightly.

15 Continue weaving to the desired length minus 1½" (3.8 cm) for the ends. **NOTE:** The finished ends measure about ¾" (1.9 cm) each. There's also some displacement caused from the weave. I typically wear a 6¼" (15.9 cm) cuff, but I made my cuff, with both ends added in, 6½" (16.5 cm) long. So how much did I weave? 6½" (16.5 cm) – 1½" (3.8 cm) (¾" [1.9 cm] both ends) = 5" (12.7 cm).

NOTE: The ends of the cuff are finished with open loops. I strongly recommend you read through the remaining directions and practice your loops, deciding what size you want, with a piece of scrap wire. Once the cuff is removed from the mandrel and one side of the cuff is finished, you cannot put it back on the mandrel to weave more if you discover you didn't weave enough! I always mark and measure a piece of scrap wire the same gauge that I'm working with so I can practice making loops and refresh my memory as to how much wire I need.

16 Remove the cuff from the mandrel. Don't cut the weaving wire tail if it's at least 1' (30.5 cm) long. This will be used to string the bead and coil the frame.

17 If you cut the weaving wire tail, cut a new 1' (30.5 cm) piece of 26-gauge wire. Coil it around the frame wire two to three times.

18 Slide a bead onto the weaving wire and coil the opposite side of the frame, securing the bead (Figure 7).

19 Use flat-nose pliers to bend each frame wire end inward just past the end of the bead (Figure 8). The angle of the bend is a personal preference, but it's important that the bends are equal and the wires cross in the center.

20 Bend the wires so they are parallel to each other (Figure 9).

21 Determine how much wire is needed to make a simple loop (page 13) with an additional one-quarter turn to create an open spiral. Measure from the bends made in Step 22 the length needed for an open spiral. Mark and flush cut the frame wire, then loop both wire ends.

22 Use the 26-gauge wire tail to coil one frame wire starting from the end of the weave to the point where the frame wires are parallel to each other. Pull the wire across the frame wires, then coil the other frame wire to the end of the weave (Figure 10).

23 Cut 8" (20.3 cm) of 26-gauge wire and coil the two looped frame wire ends together. Cut all the wire tails on this end of the cuff (Figure 11).

24 Carefully push the weave so it's tight against the finished end.

25 Cut the cuff frame wires in the corners of the bend made in Step 5, then repeat Steps 20–25 to finish the second side of the cuff.

26 Shape the cuff on a bracelet mandrel. This is best done by pushing the cuff ends around the mandrel. Remove the cuff from the mandrel and carefully bend/round the cuff ends by hand to further shape the cuff.

autumn leaf
BRACELET

Copper wirework frames a stunning copper-clad glass artisan bead, echoing an autumn theme. Incorporate your own handmade bead and matching wire to give your bracelet a unique look.

DESIGN INSPIRATION

I met an amazing lampwork/electroforming artist at the 2009 Tucson Gem and Mineral Show, Kathy Hoppe of Ogosh Buttons & Beads. I instantly fell in love with her beads, and she fell in love with my woven jewelry. She commissioned me to design a bracelet for her with one of her beads and that is when I designed the Autumn Leaf Bracelet. Kathy tells me she uses real leaves when she electroforms her beads.

PROJECT NOTES

Since the focal bead in this piece is woven to two frames, its hole needs to be large enough to handle two 22-gauge wire passes. Lampworked beads are perfect for this.

FINISHED SIZE

25 x 18 mm (ring top)

MATERIALS

1 large-holed 32mm focal bead

20" (50.8 cm) of 16-gauge dead-soft wire

16" (40.6 cm) of 22-gauge dead-soft wire

13' to 15' (4 m to 4.6 m) of 26-gauge dead-soft wire

1 handmade Woven Hook clasp (page 78)

TOOLS

Flush cutters

Permanent marking pen

Ruler

Round-nose pliers

Chain-nose pliers

Flat-nose pliers

Nylon-jaw wire-straightening pliers

Stick pin (optional)

Bracelet mandrel

Goldsmith's hammer (optional)

Metal block or anvil (optional)

Files and sandpaper (optional)

Silver Black or liver of sulfur and steel wool (optional)

TECHNIQUES USED

Wire Weaving (page 16)

Coiling (page 20)

1 Measure the combined length of the bead and the clasp. Subtract that length from the desired bracelet size. Divide that number in half. Take note of the final measurement—this is how long each frame will need to be.

2 Determine the length of wire you'll need to make the spiraled ends at the end of each frame by first cutting 3" (7.6 cm) of 16-gauge scrap wire and marking the wire at ¾" (1.9 cm), 1" (2.5 cm), and 1¼" (3.2 cm). Use the tips of round-nose pliers to form a loop on the end nearest the ¾" (1.9 cm) mark. Place the wide end of round-nose pliers under the small loop just made, with the loop facing toward you. Roll the wire until the small loop touches the 16-gauge wire. Ideally, there will be a mark at the top center of your loop. The top center of my loop falls just before the 1" (2.5 cm) mark, estimating that I use ⅞" (2.1 cm) to form my spiraled ends (Figure 1). **NOTE:** This measurement changes with every wire gauge. Be sure to always use the same gauge as your project when calculating the length of wire needed. **NOTE:** The base of the frame can be any desired width, but making it wider than 1" (2.5 cm) makes it difficult to keep the weaving wires uniform and straight. To make a wider frame, adjust the measurement in Step 2.

3 Straighten and flush cut 10" (25.4 cm) of 16-gauge wire. Mark the center of the wire. **NOTE:** This is a guiding mark only.

4 Make a mark ⅜" (9 mm) on each side of the center mark. This will make the end of each frame ¾" (1.9 cm) wide. Use flat-nose pliers to form 90° bends on each of these two marks so the wire ends point in the same direction.

5 Add the frame wire length (from Step 1) to the spiraled end length (from Step 2). Mark the wire at this measurement from the 90° bend. Flush cut the wire at this mark.

6 Use the tips of round-nose pliers to form a loop on each wire end. The loops should point toward the inside of the frame wire (Figure 2).

7 Place the wide end of round-nose pliers under one of the small loops just made. Roll the wire until the small loop touches the outside of the frame wire. Repeat for the second small loop.

8 **OPTIONAL:** Forge (page 21) and file the top curves of the large arches. Set aside.

9 Repeat Steps 3–7 to form the second frame.

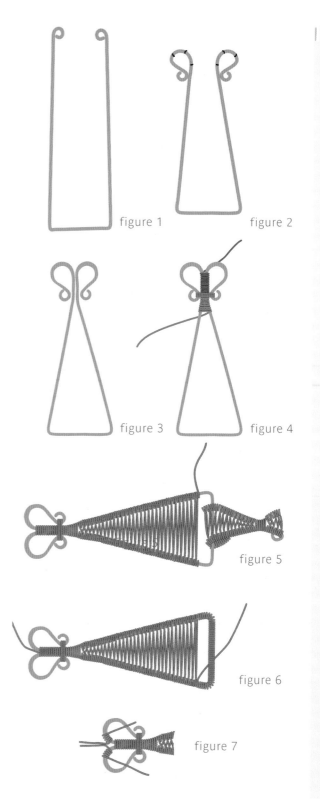

figure 1

figure 2

figure 3

figure 4

figure 5

figure 6

figure 7

1 0 Gently squeeze the wire frame together so the two spiraled ends touch each other.

1 1 Use chain-nose pliers to grasp the wire underneath one spiraled end and form a slight bend outward. Repeat this for the second hook. Gently squeeze the hooks together so the frame wires are parallel at the spiraled ends. If necessary, adjust the bends until the frame wire is parallel (Figure 3).

1 2 Cut 3' to 4' (.9 m to 1.2 m) of 26-gauge wire.

1 3 Use the 26-gauge wire to coil the two frame wires together, starting at the top inside of the spiraled ends, coiling down to the small loops (Figure 4—blue wire).

1 4 Coil three to four times inside the small loops of each spiraled end (Figure 4—red wire). **NOTE:** The small loops can be opened as you would open a jump ring, which makes it much easier to coil.

1 5 Coil the frame wires together ten to twelve more times until there's enough space to weave (Figure 4—brown wire).

1 6 Follow Weave Pattern 1 (page 16) until you reach ¼" (6 mm) from the bottom of the frame. To determine how much of the frame not to weave, slip the Woven Hook over the end of the frame wire. If necessary, add more weave, then check the fit of the Woven Hook again. A good rule of thumb is to leave the opening for the hook about the same depth as the Woven Hook's head (Figure 5).

1 7 Coil the remainder of the frame wire (Figure 6).

1 8 Carefully trim the working wire on the inside of the frame wire. Use chain-nose pliers to carefully squeeze the end of the weaving wire against the frame wire. **NOTE:** If you accidentally squeeze part of the weave, use a stick pin to straighten it.

1 9 Pull the beginning working wire tail between the two spirals, angling it up to make it easier to cut. Trim the tail flush to the frame wire, then push the wire down between the spiraled ends. Set aside.

2 0 Repeat Steps 8–17, weaving the second frame. For symmetry, weave the same length as the first frame wire side.

2 1 Cut two 6" (15.2 cm) pieces of 22-gauge wire.

2 2 Coil one piece of wire around one of the frame's spiraled ends four times. Repeat with the second piece of wire, coiling around the second spiraled end of the same frame (Figure 7).

2 3 Pass the two wires through the bead and one wire through each spiraled end on the second frame. Bend each wire back to catch the spiraled ends. The easiest way to do this is by placing all three pieces on a flat surface. Leave space, about 3 mm, between both frames and the bead, then bend the wires on the side to be coiled (Figure 8).

2 4 Coil each wire four times around each hook spiraled end. Trim any tails (Figure 9).

2 5 Cut two 3" (7.6 cm) pieces of 22-gauge wire. Coil one time around the two wires attaching the bead to the spiraled ends. Repeat this on the second side.

2 6 Again, coil one time around one side, then coil one time around the second side. Repeat this until there is no room left to coil. Trim the tails (Figure 10).

2 7 Use a bracelet mandrel or nylon-jaw bracelet-forming pliers to form the frame sides. Attach the Woven Hook to one end of the bracelet.

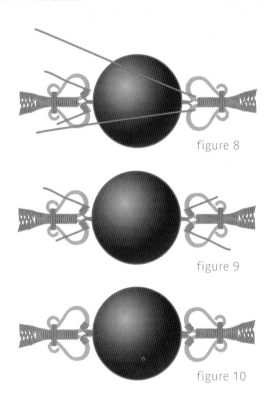

figure 8

figure 9

figure 10

○ BEGINNER

○ INTERMEDIATE

● ADVANCED

key to my steampunk
HEART

Incorporate real watch gears and crystal beads to form this woven skeleton key pendant. It's a clever combination that's dripping with Steampunk style.

DESIGN INSPIRATION

I love Steampunk jewelry! I really wanted a Steampunk piece for my book, and when I saw Lori Mendenhall's heart pendants, I immediately thought "Wow, those are awesome" and about ten seconds afterwards I thought, "Those need keys to go with them!" Lori kindly made this Steampunk heart pendant at my request and as soon as I received it in the mail, I got out my collection of antique cabinet keys, picked my favorite one, and started doodling with wire.

PROJECT NOTES

For my 6 mm mandrel I use the wide end of round-nose pliers. For the 8 mm mandrel, I use the barrel of a pen. See page 11 for other mandrel suggestions.

FINISHED SIZE

18¾" (47.6 cm)

MATERIALS

9" (22.9 cm) of 16-gauge dead-soft wire

6" (15.2 cm) of 18-gauge dead-soft wire

7' to 8' (2.1 to 2.4 m) of 26-gauge dead-soft wire

2 watch gears

2 crystal 3mm bicone beads

41" (1 m) of commercial or handmade chain (page 14)

1 heart-shaped 14mm toggle clasp or spiral hook clasp (page 15)

2 round 6mm 16-gauge jump rings (if toggle is used)

1 oval 7 x 9mm 16-gauge jump ring

1 polymer clay 35 x 43mm Steampunk-style heart pendant

Low-stick tape

Silver leafing pen (optional)

TOOLS

see page 116

TECHNIQUES USED

Coiling (page 20)

Wire Weaving (page 16)

TOOLS

Flush cutters

Old pair of flush cutters

Round-nose pliers

6 mm mandrel

8 mm mandrel

Chain-nose pliers

Flat-nose pliers

Nylon-jaw wire-
straightening pliers

Ruler

Permanent marking pen

Metal needle file or
reamer (optional)

1   Straighten and cut 9" (22.9 cm) of 16-gauge wire. This is
    the key frame wire.

2   Use the pen to mark the center of the wire, then mark 8
    mm on each side of the center mark. Mark 20 mm from
    each of the 8 mm marks.

3   Make 90° bends on the two 8 mm marks.

4   Hold the 6 mm mandrel on the center mark between the
    8 mm marks made in Step 2 and pull each side of the wire
    around the mandrel, making a half circle in between the
    two 8 mm marks (Figure 1—red wire).

5   Hold the 8 mm mandrel next to one of the bends made in
    Step 5, then make a one-quarter turn. Pull the wire the rest
    of the way around the mandrel, making a half circle. The
    more the wire is rolled as opposed to pulled, the more the
    90° bend gets rolled out (Figure 1—gray wire).

6   Use flat-nose pliers to make a 90° bend on the 20 mm
    mark made in Step 2 (Figure 2).

7   Repeat Steps 5–6 on the second side of the key frame wire
    (Figure 3).

8   Measuring from the top of the key frame wire, mark the
    left frame wire at 2" (5.1 cm), then make a 90° bend on this
    mark (Figure 4). **NOTE:** This is the final length of the key.

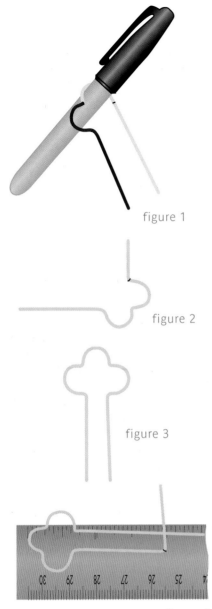

figure 1

figure 2

figure 3

figure 4

figure 5

If desired, make your key longer, but first read through the rest of the steps as there needs to be ample key frame wire left to make loops on the two wire ends.

9 Mark the left key frame wire where it crosses over the right key frame wire.

10 Measuring from the bottom of the left key frame wire, mark the right key frame wire at ⅜" (9 mm) (Figure 5).

11 Use flat-nose pliers to make a 90° bend on the right key frame wire on the mark made in Step 10 (Figure 6).

12 Use flat-nose pliers to make a 90° bend on the left key frame wire on the mark made in Step 9 (Figure 7).

13 Mark the left key frame wire next to the right key frame wire. Make a 90° bend on this mark so the two frame wire ends are parallel to each other (Figure 8).

14 Determine how much wire you'll need to finish the key frame wire ends. You can form simple loops, tight or open spirals, or a half turn—your choice! Whatever you decide, the loops or spirals need to stop short of the stem of the key by at least ⅛" (3 mm). **NOTE:** I strongly recommend you decide and practice making the end of the key frame wire first on a scrap piece of 16-gauge wire. I always mark and measure a piece of scrap wire the same gauge that I'm working with for the final piece in order to practice making my loops and to refresh my memory as to how much wire I need.

   Flush cut the key frame wire ends to the appropriate length needed, then make a loop or spiral on each end of the wire ends.

15 Straighten and cut 6" (15.2 cm) of 18-gauge wire. This is the filigree frame wire. Use the pen to mark the center of the wire, then make a 90° bend on the mark.

16 To determine where to make the second 90° bend, place the filigree frame wire over the key frame wire with the bend at the inside bottom. Use the pen to mark the wire so that once the bend is made, it will fit inside the key frame with space for weaving between the two frame wires on both sides. The spacing will be minimal, only about 1 mm. Make a 90° bend on this mark (Figure 9).

17 With the filigree frame wire inside the key frame wire, mark both sides of the wire where the key frame curves out. Make 90° bends on these marks (Figure 10).

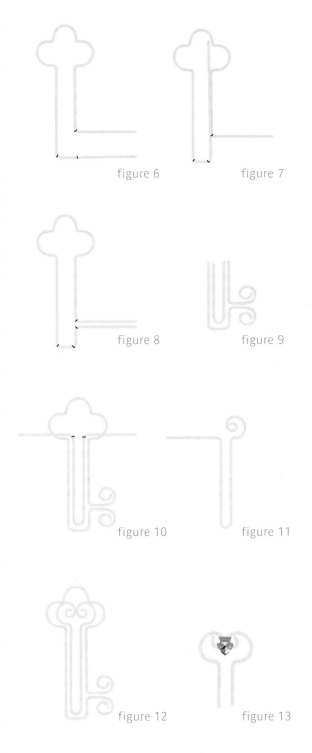

figure 6   figure 7

figure 8   figure 9

figure 10   figure 11

figure 12   figure 13

18 Hold the 6 mm mandrel at the 90° bend, then make a one-quarter turn or less—remember, the more the wire is rolled, the more the bend rolls out. Pull the wire the rest of the way around the mandrel, making a half circle.

19 Determine how much wire you need to make a loop with an additional quarter turn. This loop needs to stop short of the half circle made in Step 18 by at least ⅛" (3 mm). Measure from the curve of the half circle, adding in ⅛" (3 mm), then mark the wire for cutting. Flush cut the frame wire end and form a small loop on the end of the filigree frame wire (Figure 11).

20 Repeat Step 18. For ease of creating the loop in Step 21, open the filigree wire at the base as you would open a jump ring.

21 Repeat Step 19 on the second filigree frame wire end (Figure 12).

22 Cut 6" (15.2 cm) of 26-gauge wire. Coil the two small loops of the filigree frame wire together three to four times.

23 Coil one small loop three to four times, then string 1 bead onto the wire.

24 Coil the second small loop three to four times, then cut both 26-gauge wire tails (Figure 13).

25 Place the filigree frame inside the key frame on a flat surface. When positioned appropriately, tape the top and bottom of the two frames together. **NOTE:** As you weave, the tape won't hold your frames in place. Be sure to check them periodically to ensure alignment.

26 Cut 4' (1.2 m) of 26-gauge wire. Coil the two looped ends (the key's "notch") of the key frame wire together twelve to fourteen times, then coil around the curve of the key frame wire four to five times (Figure 14).

27 Work Weave Pattern 1 (page 16) to weave the key and filigree frame wires together up to about ⅛" (3 mm) before the first curve of the frames (Figure 15).

28 When the frames are not parallel to each other, the frame with the wider curve or bend will require more wire coiled around it and therefore requires a slightly different weave by either coiling the weaving wire more or less times around the frame wires.

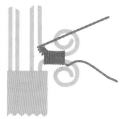

figure 14

figure 15

figure 16

figure 17

figure 18

figure 19

figure 20

As you weave your way around the top of the filigree and key frame wires, the coils required for your individual key will vary. For example, for the first corner of my key, I coiled the weaving wire two times around the key frame but coiled three times around the filigree frame. The goal is to keep the weaving straight between the two frames, not angled. Do what works for your key until the weave is about ⅛" (3 mm) past the corner (Figure 16).

2 9 When the frames are parallel, continue to work Weave Pattern 1. Where the frames are curved, adjust the weave as necessary by adding a coil or two to a frame or coiling one less time around a frame. For example, around the center of the key I needed to wrap the filigree frame wire just one time, so I didn't even make a full coil. Then I coiled the key frame three times. Continue weaving to base of the top curve of the key frame wire (Figure 17).

3 0 Coil around the top of the key frame wire, then weave one time to the filigree frame wire, bringing the weaving wire up on the right side of the weave.

3 1 Coil around the top of the filigree frame. Pull the weaving wire straight across where the two filigree loops are coiled together, then continue coiling the second loop. Trim the weaving wire tail (Figure 18).

3 2 Cut 4' (1.2 m) of 26-gauge wire. Attach the wire to the top of the key wire frame where you stopped weaving in Step 30. Continue weaving the two frame wires together, repeating Step 29, down to the first bottom corner of the two frame wires.

3 3 The weaving will need to be adjusted when weaving around the bottom two corners of the key as done in Step 29. I find it best to coil around the key frame three times and to wrap the weaving wire just one time around the filigree frame.

3 4 Continue wrapping up to the beginning coil done in Step 26 (Figure 19).

3 5 If your weave ends on the key frame wire, weave back to the filigree frame wire. Coil the filigree frame wire two to three times, leaving bare filigree frame wire to attach the bead and gears.

3 6 Trim the ending weaving wire tail. Before trimming the beginning wire tail from Step 26, use it to tighten the coil. Set the key aside.

3 7 If necessary, trim any sharp screws, bolts, or pins from the watch gears. It can be pulled out with chain-nose pliers but may need to be trimmed with old flush cutters; just place the cutters flush against the gear and cut. You may need to cut on both sides of the gear. If desired, paint the gear silver using the leafing pen.

3 8 Cut 6" (15.2 cm) of 26-gauge wire. Make a 90° bend at 3" (7.6 cm), then slide a bead onto the wire. Bend the wire on the other side of the bead.

3 9 Slide a gear or two onto the wire, threading both wire ends through the gears. If the holes in the gears are too tiny to get wire through, stick the tip of a metal needle file or reamer into the hole and turn it back and forth a few times to make the holes larger (Figure 20).

4 0 String the two wire ends through the opening between the key frame and the filigree frame and coil the wires around the filigree frame one time, pulling both wires tightly. Next, bring one or both wire ends around the coiled key notch one time. Feed the wires back around the filigree frame wire. To continue to coil the wires around the filigree frame wire, you'll need to feed the wires up through the gears, then back down through the gears on the opposite side of the filigree frame. Do this two to three times as you can. Cut the wire tails.

4 1 Attach the oval jump ring to the top of the key. Slide the chain through the jump ring and the heart pendant.

4 2 Use 1 jump ring to connect the chain ends to one half of the clasp. Use 1 jump ring to connect the other clasp half 19" (48.3 cm) down the chain.

BEGINNER

INTERMEDIATE

● ADVANCED

melonia's
CROSS

Create this intricate piece by coiling and weaving heart frames together into a cross shape. The result is a stunning jewel-encrusted pendant that evokes vintage filigree.

DESIGN INSPIRATION

I wanted to make a woven wire cross in honor of one of my grandmothers. While playing with some design ideas, my cross evolved into this filigree necklace.

PROJECT NOTES

The coin bead hole needs to be large enough to accommo-date two passes of 26-gauge wire. The size of your briolettes depends on what fits with your heart frames. The best thing to do is to make the frames, then lay everything out to make sure everything fits.

As with the Coiled Heart Necklace (page 62), shaping your hearts may take a few practice runs. Try shaping a heart first with craft, brass, or copper wire before using sterling silver.

FINISHED SIZE

18" (45.7 cm)

MATERIALS

2' 3" (68.6 m) of 16-gauge dead-soft wire

14' (4.3 m) of 26-gauge dead-soft wire

4 glass, crystal, or stone 8 x 11mm flat top-drilled briolettes

1 crystal 6mm coin bead

8 crystal 3mm round or bicone beads

16" (40.6 cm) of commer-cial or handmade chain (page 14)

1 toggle clasp or hand-made 26mm spiral hook clasp (page 15)

4 round 6mm 16-gauge jump rings (if toggle or commercial chain is used)

Low-stick tape

TOOLS

see page 122

TECHNIQUES USED

Coiling (page 20)

Wire Weaving (page 16)

TOOLS

Flush cutters

Round-nose pliers

Chain-nose pliers

Flat-nose pliers

Nylon-jaw wire-
straightening pliers

Nylon-jaw bracelet-
forming pliers

Ruler

Permanent marking pen

figure 1

figure 2

figure 3 figure 4

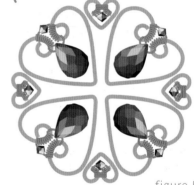

figure 5

figure 6

1   Follow Steps 1–5 of the Coiled Heart Necklace, (page 62) to make four large heart frames. In order for the 3mm bead to fit in the center of the two heart halves, leave a small space between the halves. Also, leave the two small loops made in Step 3 slightly open to facilitate coiling.

2   Cut 8" (20.3 cm) of 26-gauge wire. Coil two times above a small loop on one of the heart frames, then string a 3mm bead onto the wire.

3   Coil two times above the second small loop, then coil six to eight times inside the small loop. String a briolette onto the wire (Figure 1).

4   Coil inside the second small loop to mirror the number of coils you created in Step 3. Cut both wire tails (Figure 2). Set the large heart frame aside.

5   Repeat Steps 2– 4 for the remaining three heart frames.

6   Straighten and flush cut 1¼" (3.2 cm) of 16-gauge wire. Use the pen to mark the wire's center.

7   Use flat-nose pliers to form a V-shaped bend at the mark.

8   Use the tips of round-nose pliers to form a loop at each wire end that faces in toward the V.

9   Repeat Steps 6–8 for the remaining three mini-heart frames.

10 Cut 1' (30.5 cm) of 26-gauge wire. Coil the two small loops of a mini-heart frame together three times (Figure 3).

1 1 Coil one small loop below the coil created in Step 10 two times, then string a 3mm bead onto the wire.

1 2 Coil around the second small loop, securing the bead. Coil up to the bottom of the center coil made in Step 10, coiling two times to mirror the coils from Step 11. Cut both wire tails and gently squeeze the ends down with chain-nose pliers (Figure 4). Set the mini-heart frame aside.

1 3 Repeat Steps 11–12 for the remaining three mini-heart frames.

1 4 Lay the heart frames in the pattern shown to form a cross shape (Figure 5). **NOTE:** The large heart tips should not touch in the center when determining the size of the outer frame as there needs to be room for weaving.

1 5 Straighten and flush cut 8" (20.3 cm) of 16-gauge wire. Use nylon-jaw bracelet-forming pliers to shape the wire into a circle, starting at one end and working your way to the second wire end. This is the outer frame.

1 6 For this step and Step 25, you need to know how much wire you use to make a simple loop (page 13). Form a simple loop on one wire end (Figure 6).

1 7 Lay the outer frame over the cross shape to check the sizing. The arches of all the hearts should touch or almost touch the outer frame. If the frame needs to be smaller, gently push the two wire ends until they overlap each other by about ½" (1.3 cm) on each side. Hold the wire ends where they overlap and use nylon-jaw bracelet-forming pliers to reshape the wire into a circle.

1 8 Repeat Step 17 until the outer frame fits appropriately around the heart frames. **NOTE:** Final sizing to the outer frame will be done in Steps 25–27 (Figure 7).

1 9 For ease of working with the outer frame, slightly open the frame as you would a jump ring.

2 0 Cut 6' (1.8 m) of 26-gauge wire. Leaving a 2" (5.1 cm) tail, coil three times next to the loop made in Step 16, then string the wire through the right-sided small loop of a mini heart. **NOTE:** Don't push the coils tightly together as the heart frames are added. There needs to be leeway in the coil for sizing and adjusting the alignment of all the heart frames in Steps 25–27.

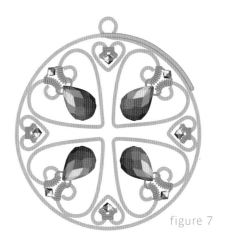

figure 7

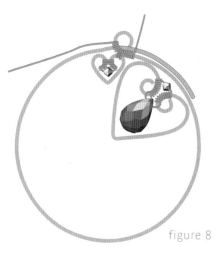

figure 8

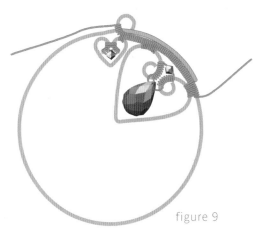

figure 9

21 Coil the mini-heart arch two to three times, then coil the outer frame three to four times. The center of this mini heart should be lined up with the center of the outer frame loops. (The second frame loop will be connected in Step 25.) Lay the frame on a flat surface, then place a large heart inside the outer frame wire next to the mini heart. Use the pen to mark the outer frame wire where the heart arch will be attached (Figure 8).

22 Coil the outer frame up to the pen mark. Coil the heart arch seven to nine times, the outer frame between the heart arches, and the second heart arch to mirror the number of coils on the first heart arch (Figure 9).

23 Coil the remainder of the small and large hearts to the outer frame.

24 Push the outer frame wire together to determine where the small heart added in Step 20 will be attached and mark the outer frame. Coil to this mark, then coil the first mini heart's second loop to fully attach it (Figure 10).

25 To make the second simple loop, measure the non-looped end of the outer frame from the back of the first loop, marking the wire to the figure determined in Step 16. Flush cut the wire on this mark.

26 Form the second simple loop.

27 Align the center of the mini-heart frame by pushing the coil on the outer frame wire away from the two center loops on both sides until the mini-heart frame is centered between the two outer frame loops (Figure 11).

28 Coil as necessary to the base of the two loops on the outer frame, then coil the two loops together.

29 Use the beginning 2" (5.1 cm) 26-gauge wire tail to coil up to the base of the two loops on the outer frame. Trim all 26-gauge wire tails (Figure 12).

30 If any of the heart frames are sitting cockeyed, use flat-nose pliers to grasp each side of it and push up or pull down until the heart is aligned. Doing this repositions the heart arches within the coil where the heart frame is attached to the outer frame. Coils on the outer frame can also be pushed or pulled to help with alignment.

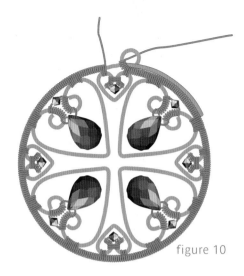

figure 10

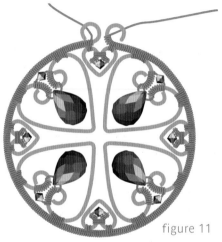

figure 11

figure 12

31 Cut 4' (1.2 m) of 26-gauge wire. Leaving a 2' (61 cm) tail, coil around the tip of one heart frame twice. String the coin bead onto the wire, then coil around the tip of the opposite heart frame twice (Figure 13).

32 Work Weave Pattern 1 to connect two heart frames together. Weave back and forth only twice, then use the 2' (61 cm) tail to weave between the second two heart frames twice. Take care to not pull the frames out of alignment while weaving.

33 Cut 4' (1.2 m) of 26-gauge wire. Leaving a 2' (61 cm) tail, coil twice next to the coil around the heart frame tip from Step 31. String the wire through the center bead, then coil twice around the second heart frame tip from Step 31.

34 Repeat Step 32 on the second two heart frames (Figure 14).

35 Continue weaving between the heart frames twice, then move to the next weave and weave twice. Weaving between each frame a small amount at a time keeps the weave length uniform. Check the alignment of the heart frames as necessary. Weave up to the bottom of the mini hearts' tips.

36 Coil three to four times along the side of a large heart frame, then coil fifteen to twenty times around the mini-heart tip, attaching the large and small heart frames together.

37 Coil three to four times along the side of the opposing large heart frame, back to the weave (Figure 15). Cut the wire tail.

38 Repeat Steps 36–37 for the remaining three mini-heart frames.

39 Cut the chain into two 8" (20.3 cm) pieces. Attach one chain to each loop on the outer frame.

40 Connect the clasp to the chain ends.

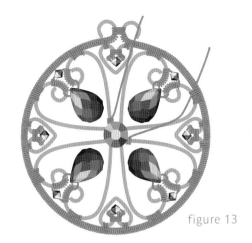

figure 13

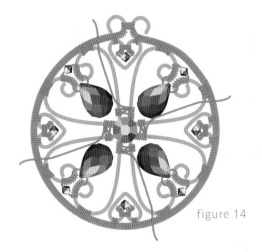

figure 14

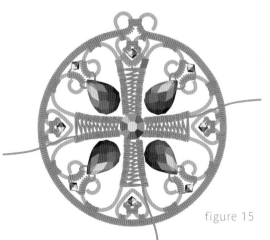

figure 15

RESOURCES

Wire

Parawire
parawire.com
2-8 Central Ave.
East Orange, NJ 07018
(973) 672-0500

Indian Jewelers Supply
ijsinc.com
601 East Coal Ave.
Gallup, NM 87301
(800) 545-6540

Starr Gems
silversupplies.com
220 West Drachman St.
Tucson, AZ 85705
(520) 882-8750

Findings

Tierra Cast
Check your local bead store or
favorite online store

Fusion Beads
fusionbeads.com
13024 Stone Ave. N.
Seattle, WA 98133
(888) 781-3559

Watch Gears

MisterArt
misterart.com
(800) 721-3015

Sterling, Hill Tribe, and Thai Silver Beads

Ands Silver
andssilver.com
PO Box 411465
Los Angeles, CA 90041
(323) 254-5250

Kalpataru Beads Inc.
kalpatarubeads.com
314 5th Ave., 5th Fl.
New York, NY 10001
(917) 330-1717

Semiprecious Stone Beads

Bead Palace Inc.
beadpalaceinc.com
163 South Madison Ave.
Greenwood, IN 46142
(317) 882-9392

TAJ Company
tajcompany.com
42 West 48th St.
New York, NY 10036
(212) 944-6330

Crystals

ABC Direct Importers
349 East Fort Lowell
Tucson, AZ 85705
(877) 696-9490

Julie Designer Group Inc.
2595 Pomona Blvd.
Pomona, CA 91768
(818) 674-7669

Venetian Glass Beads

Venetian Bead Shop
venetianbeadshop.com
1010 Stewart Dr.
Sunnyvale, CA 94085
(800) 439-3551

Bella Venetian Beads
bellavenetianbeads.com
424 Fort Hill Dr., Ste. 102
Naperville, IL 60540
(630) 416-2345

Artisan Beads

Kathy Hoppe
O'Gosh Buttons & Beads
OhGosh-Buttons.com
2411 Doty St.
Oshkosh, WI 54902

Becklin Bead Designs
BecklinBeadDesigns.com
(832) 334-9371

Lori Mendenhall
Lori Mendenhall Jewelry Studio
lorimendenhall.com
lorimendenhall@cox.net

ACKNOWLEDGMENTS

Thanks to Denise Peck, editor of *Step By Step Wire Jewelry* magazine, who has always believed in me and given me confidence. To Tricia Waddell for giving me this opportunity and, like Denise, having confidence in me to pull it off.

To my children, Joanna, Jules, and Joey. How can a mom ever put into words what her children mean to her? They think what I do is "so cool" and they are very proud of me. Of course, they get all the free jewelry they want, and they always want whatever is the newest thing hot off the jewelry bench. I adore them. They are my life's best accomplishment!

Thanks to my sisters, Charli and Misti, and my parents, for all the support you have given.

Finally, thanks to my dear friends Lis Swebe-Cook, Abby Hook, Lori Mendenhall, Franchezka Westwood, and Eni Oken. Couldn't have done it without you ladies!

INDEX

Learn more innovative wire techniques with these inspiring resources from Interweave

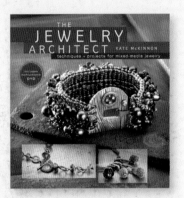

THE JEWELRY ARCHITECT
Techniques + Projects for Mixed-Media Jewelry
Kate McKinnon
ISBN 978-1-59668-176-7
$26.95

WIRE STYLE
50 Unique Jewelry Designs
Denise Peck
ISBN 978-1-59668-070-8
$19.95

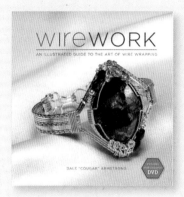

WIREWORK
An Illustrated Guide to the Art of Wire Wrapping
Dale "Cougar" Armstrong
ISBN 978-1-59668-290-0
$26.95

Join JewelryMakingDaily.com, an online community that shares your passion for jewelry. You'll get a free e-newsletter, free projects, a daily blog, a pattern store, galleries, artist interviews, contests, tips and techniques, and more. Sign up for *Jewelry Making Daily* at jewelrymakingdaily.com.

Check out *Jewelry Artist,* a trusted guide to the art of gems, jewelry making, design, beads, minerals, and more. Whether you are a beginner, an experienced artisan, or in the jewelry business, *Jewelry Artist* can take you to a whole new level.

INTERWEAVE.
interweave.com